Editor-in-Chief and Founder:
Lyndon H. LaRouche, Jr.
Editorial Board: *Lyndon H. LaRouche, Jr. , Helga Zepp-LaRouche, Paul Gallagher, Tony Papert, Gerald Rose, Dennis Small, Jeffrey Steinberg, William Wertz*
Co-Editors: *Paul Gallagher, Tony Papert*
Managing Editor: *Nancy Spannaus*
Technology: *Marsha Freeman*
Books: *Katherine Notley*
Graphics: *Alan Yue*
Photos: *Stuart Lewis*
Circulation Manager: *Stanley Ezrol*

INTELLIGENCE DIRECTORS
Counterintelligence: *Jeffrey Steinberg, Michele Steinberg*
Economics: *John Hoefle, Marcia Merry Baker, Paul Gallagher*
History: *Anton Chaitkin*
Ibero-America: *Dennis Small*
Russia and Eastern Europe: *Rachel Douglas*
United States: *Debra Freeman*

INTERNATIONAL BUREAUS
Bogotá: *Miriam Redondo*
Berlin: *Rainer Apel*
Copenhagen: *Tom Gillesberg*
Houston: *Harley Schlanger*
Lima: *Sara Madueño*
Melbourne: *Robert Barwick*
Mexico City: *Gerardo Castilleja Chávez*
New Delhi: *Ramtanu Maitra*
Paris: *Christine Bierre*
Stockholm: *Ulf Sandmark*
United Nations, N.Y.C.: *Leni Rubinstein*
Washington, D.C.: *William Jones*
Wiesbaden: *Göran Haglund*

ON THE WEB
e-mail: eirns@larouchepub.com
www.larouchepub.com
www.executiveintelligencereview.com
www.larouchepub.com/eiw
Webmaster: *John Sigerson*
Assistant Webmaster: *George Hollis*
Editor, Arabic-language edition: *Hussein Askary*

EIR (ISSN 0273-6314) *is published weekly (50 issues), by EIR News Service, Inc., P.O. Box 17390, Washington, D.C. 20041-0390. (703) 777-9451*

European Headquarters: E.I.R. GmbH, Postfach Bahnstrasse 9a, D-65205, Wiesbaden, Germany Tel: 49-611-73650
Homepage: http://www.eirna.com
e-mail: eirna@eirna.com
Director: Georg Neudecker

Montreal, Canada: 514-461-1557

Denmark: EIR - Danmark, Sankt Knuds Vej 11, basement left, DK-1903 Frederiksberg, Denmark. Tel.: +45 35 43 60 40, Fax: +45 35 43 87 57. e-mail: eirdk@hotmail.com.

Mexico City: EIR, Sor Juana Inés de la Cruz 242-2 Col. Agricultura C.P. 11360
Delegación M. Hidalgo, México D.F.
Tel. (5525) 5318-2301
eirmexico@gmail.com

Postmaster: Send all address changes to *EIR*, P.O. Box 17390, Washington, D.C. 20041-0390.

The Obama Murders

EIR Contents

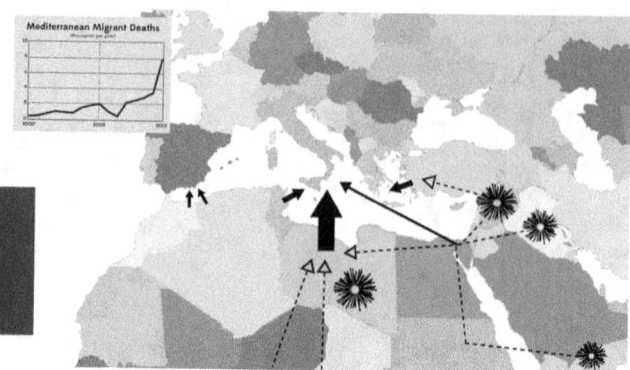

EIRNS/Spencer Cross

Cover This Week

Mediterranean migrant deaths

www.larouchepub.com   Volume 42, Number 18, May 1, 2015

I. The Obama Murders

April 22—Notable today and recently, are the drownings off the Mediterranean coasts, on a massive scale.

But we also have, to complement that, from California in particular, a threat of massive depopulation.

What this indicates is that we have a global trend, especially in certain parts of the world,—to reduce the population drastically. And this includes not only the carnage which Obama actually created by his reign of terror in North Africa, but it has also been flooding the waters of the Mediterranean with mass drownings of people desperately fleeing everywhere,—anywhere,—to escape the reach of the protégés of Obama.

And you see that the same thing is happening in California,—but we know it's not limited to there. We know there's a trend, throughout the United States in particular, and as in this Mediterranean region, where mass extermination of the human population is under way. And what we're seeing in the mass drownings and similar things in the Mediterranean coming from Africa, and what we're seeing as threatened in California, are the same thing.

This scheme has the support of, particularly, the current President of the United States, Obama. This genocide policy, which is reflected by the policymaking of Obama among others, is what faces mankind now.

The crisis in the Mediterranean Sea, comes largely from the area that was destroyed when first Bush, and then Obama far more, changed its regimes, or tried to. Obama was the one who created the chaos which we now see reflected in the flight into being drowned, among thousands of people in especially the central part of the Mediterranean Sea.

So therefore, Obama is something which must be removed,—must be stopped,—because he's morally an enemy of humanity. And what his policies are, are those of the enemy of humanity.

The Truth of the Matter

What can you say about all the suckers who don't know any better, who still think that Obama's a real person?—They should ask what his mama did for a living. That might help them understand things better. Like his predecessor the Roman Emperor Nero, Obama chose the wrong mother.

But, regardless,—this is the issue. We cannot accept the opinion of people who support Obama! Because the evidence is in plain view for anybody with intelligence,—or active intelligence,—to see that Obama is a disease! He's not a President; he's a disease disguised as a President. And only when you talk that way, do you get to the truth of the matter.

We're dealing with a real form of Nazism, beyond anything that Hitler tried, and it's coming from the trans-Atlantic community, or elements of the trans-Atlantic community.

Murder in the Mediterranean

by EIR Staff

April 24—The evidence is clear: The Barack Obama who now comments, distant and seemingly uninvolved, on the death of 900 migrants in a single boat, is the murderer quietly viewing the scene of his crime, while media investigators scurry about pointing fingers at Europe. And his crime is not the murder of these 900 only.

It is Obama's jihadi killers in Libya—the ones who have shot and bombed their way into power in Tripoli since the Obama/British "regime change" bombing and invasion of 2011—who are behind the boat smuggling operations in which unknown thousands of migrants have died at sea. The U.S. assassination of Muammar Qaddafi ("We came, we saw: He died," intoned Obama Secretary of State Hillary Clinton over Qaddafi's corpse) turned the former state of Libya into the fountainhead of terrorism for all of North Africa, the Sahel, and even Syria. Now the "winners" of Obama's murder sweepstakes in Tripoli, are organizing the herding of refugees onto boats to drown by the thousands. "The Mediterranean is being made a cemetery," cried Pope Francis, and it is Obama and British Prime Minister David Cameron who laid it waste.

Moreover: The same Obama crime, then abetted by his close friend at the time, President Recep Tayyip Erdogan of Turkey, brought Islamic jihadis armed from Libya's weapon stores into Syria; and with the growth of the Islamic State (ISIS), into Iraq. Hundreds of thousands of refugees from *those* countries as well, trying now to reach Europe, have found themselves at the mercy of the Tripoli jihadi command which Obama fostered.

Consider the great debate over "responsibility" now going on among European governments, as a discussion of how to deal with the growing numbers of victims of Obama's (and Cameron's) crime of unleashing and arming terrorism throughout the Mediterranean region. Justice for this war policy by the great Nobel Peace Prize winner in the White House, begins by throwing him out of it.

'Saving Benghazi'

On the weekend of April 18-19, between 700 and 900 African migrants reportedly died in one of the largest shipwrecks in modern times in Libyan territorial waters. Since the start of 2014, the *Los Angeles Times* reports, there have been about 4,400 boat deaths of migrants coming from Libya—with 900 so far in 2015 *before* the latest incident. Some estimates say 20,000 have drowned, among 200,000 fleeing migrants.

These and other deaths as a result of the 2011 Libya War are not "collateral" damage—they were the intent. It was Obama and the British who rammed through the UN Security Council resolution in 2011, in the name of saving Libyan civilians from a "humanitarian" disaster in Benghazi; it was Obama and Cameron who lied to the UNSC, saying there was no plan for regime change; then a U.S.-U.K.-led military coalition eventually started the regime change by bombing Libya. For specific reasons which might have to do with his election campaign funding, French President Nicholas Sarkozy inaugurated the air strikes, informing his EU partners after the attack had started. And it was French Intelligence under Sarkozy which led rebels to capture and murder Qaddafi.

It was Obama, Britain, and the Saudi and Qatari Wahhabis who put the al-Qaeda-affiliated Libyan Islamic Fighting Group (LIFG)'s people into power, and later ran the ratline of arms from Libya to Syria, which built up al-Nusra and the Islamic State.

When U.S., U.K., and French bombers and special forces "saved" the city of Benghazi from an imminent advance of Qaddafi's armed forces in 2011, they were saving the powers in that city who had sent a greater proportion of foreign jihadis to fight U.S. forces in Iraq since 2003, than any other region.

White House/Pete Souza

Obama's jihadi killers are the same people who are smuggling migrants out of Libya, thousands of whom have met their deaths at sea. Left: a ship carrying more than 1,000 refugees who were rescued in the Mediterranean.

UNHCR/F. Malavolta

The Obama Administration is effectively repeating that criminal folly today with its Saudi ally, saving al-Qaeda in Yemen from the Houthi rebel forces who were in the process of defeating al-Qaeda until Saudi Arabia started bombing with Obama's active backing. Al-Qaeda in Yemen is consequently expanding its murderous operations—the constant result of *all* Obama's actions around the Mediterranean.

The Muslim Brotherhood/al-Qaeda forces that Obama "saved" in Benghazi (generally run by the LIFG of Abdel-Hakim Belhaj) went on to spawn and link up with other militias in chaotic Libya, murdering Americans at the Benghazi consulate in 2012, setting up terrorist training bases in the south and east of the country, and running weapons to Syria and Iraq. After Libyans elected a representative government in 2014, the LIFG and Muslim Brotherhood took over Tripoli, and forced the elected government to flee to Tobruk on the Egyptian border. Tripoli's "mayor," Maydi al-Harati, led an al-Qaeda force of 600 jihadis in Syria.

Obama's White House now insists that Libya's elected government, in exile in Tobruk, must negotiate with the murderers in Tripoli to form a new government.

These are the same jihadi killers who are now profiteering by herding people onto the ships of death.

Obama's and al-Qaeda's Mediterranean

The Italian daily *Il Giornale*'s war correspondent Gian Micalessin, in an April 20 analysis, pointed to the Obama Administration-backed Tripoli "government," as the entity running the traffic of human beings through the Mediterranean.

Since last August, when the Fajr Libya (Libyan Dawn, part of LIFG) jihadist militia took power in Tripoli, the Tripoli gang has been running the migrant racket, for purposes of financing its war against the elected government in Tobruk, Micalessin reports.

Fajr Libya is dominated by the Muslim Brotherhood and by former members of the LIFG. Tripoli has "intense relationships" with the jihadist militias that run the human trafficking at the southern Libyan borders with Sudan, Chad, and Niger. Since August, those militias have had a green light from the Tripoli gang to move tens of thousands of human beings through the desert, to the northern coast of Libya. The southern smugglers get $800 for each migrant, and the northern smugglers charge another $1,500 apiece. The "load" that sank on April 19 ensured an income of $900,000, Micalessin says, and the money is shared between the smugglers and the Fajr Libya leadership in Tripoli.

Micalessin writes that the jihadi "coalition" not only has support from Qatar and Turkey, but is also close to Ansar al-Sharia, a terrorist organization already "very close to the Islamic State." Ansar al-Sharia was the leading jihadi group in the attack that killed U.S. Ambassador Chris Stevens and three other Americans on Sept. 11, 2012, the anniversary of the 9/11 Saudi-backed terror attack in 2001.

A European Union emergency meeting called to address the migrants issue on April 23, reiterated support for Obama's UN-sponsored "negotiation" between the Tripoli terrorists and the Tobruk government. This, although all EU governments know the truth about the Tripoli gang.

That same meeting also failed to come up with any serious measures to either save human lives, or solve the roots of the migrants crisis. The EU refused to revive the successful Italian "Mare Nostrum" operation, which had rescued over 100,000 migrants from October 2013 to Nov. 1, 2014. Instead, it increased funding for the current "Triton" operation, which is a border-patrol mission operating within EU territorial borders.

Furthermore, the EU failed to adopt a change in its current immigration laws, which do not allow immigrants to reside in countries other than their country of arrival. This puts an enormous strain on Italy, the main target of migrant ships, and on bankrupt Greece. The most they could agree on, was that EU member countries can host contingents of immigrants "on a voluntary basis." For the rest, the EU will repatriate "unauthorized economic migrants to countries of origin and transit," as the final communiqué states.

How this will be implemented is an open question. Most hypocritical was Prime Minister Cameron, who offered British ships for the Triton operation, under the condition that rescued migrants are not brought to Britain! This is the same Cameron who is personally co-responsible for the immense human tragedy unfolding in Libya and northern Africa.

Furthermore, the EU Council has given a mandate to EU High Representative Federica Mogherini, to explore ways to destroy smugglers' ships in Libyan ports, before they sail. This will hardly be possible, as international law prescribes that such operations require a UN mandate (possible) and an agreement with the target country (impossible).

The other root of the crisis—poverty—has not been addressed by the EU leaders. And yet, the fact that the 900 who died in the shipwreck on April 18 were coming from Sub-Saharan Africa (the Sahel region), identifies, in poverty and hunger, a clear cause of the problem. This is the area infested by Boko Haram terrorists, but there is at least a three-decades-long history of migrations from the Sahel to Northern Africa and to Europe, due to poverty caused by desertification.

Conscious Depopulation

Helga Zepp-LaRouche commented on the situation in a webcast on April 22 (translated from German):

I see here in one glance, in the reactions to this situation, two completely different systems, two completely different paradigms. One, is really a form of a new fascism. One really has to see the absolutely cynical manner in which the EU replaced this Mare Nostrum program, maintained by Italy alone for the past year, with a program which no longer makes the attempt to save refugees from the Mediterranean Sea, but which rather says with complete cynicism, "The more of you who drown, the more the terror for those who will then be too frightened to come." That is really the total moral bankruptcy of this EU.... We knowingly let thousands of human beings drown, to defend Fortress Europe somehow.

This is being done in the same spirit as the destruction of the Greek economy by the Troika, in full awareness that the death rate in that country will be increased; the same thing can be seen in Italy, Spain, and Portugal. And it is the same spirit which blocks real development, which simply refuses real help—to Africa in general. You see this inhuman behavior, which even accepts depopulation, reduction of population; so that if you take all these aspects together, you are forced to suspect that this is exactly the intention—namely, to cut the population down.

—*Claudio Celani, Michele Steinberg, Paul Gallagher*

Obama's Mommy: What Did She Do for a Living?

by Brent Bedford

Slide 1

Slide 2

Slide 3

Brent Bedford of the LaRouche Political Action Committee gave this slide show on Nov. 16, 2011 in Northern Virginia; it has never been published before. Given the nature of the medium, some of the slides are unavoidably blurry. This version is slightly edited.

What I'm going to summarize is a series of articles by Wayne Madsen. They are from the "Wayne Madsen Report." He's a former naval intelligence officer, and so he knows some things. He knows how to read these things, and he's done a profile on Obama's background, which is probably better than "Obama on the Couch," if you want to understand why he's got some of the problems he has.

The Father

(**Slide 1**)—There's Barack Obama's father. This is Barack Obama senior.

What do people know about him? I'm just curious. The father of your President,—what can you tell me about him?

He was from Kenya. He was an alcoholic. That's what you hear about him. He met Obama's mother (Stanley Ann Dunham) in 1959, in a Russian language class. Two young people, studying the Russian language, fell in love, had a kid.... And then he left, around one year after, and Obama never saw his father again. [Except for a reported brief visit to Hawaii when Barack Obama, Jr., was eleven.]

Comment: But he was already married and had a kid before he met Obama's momma.

Yes, he was already married. When he left, he went to Harvard, and married another lady, and had a kid with her, and brought her back to Kenya.

Now, Kenyans didn't just come to American universities in 1959. That was not really done, *except...* What was happening was that a lot of African na-

Slide 4

Slide 5

Slide 6

Slide 7

tions were getting their independence from British colonial rule, and the CIA decided that we should... The CIA brought over 280 East African and South African students, to attend American universities, and become CIA agents, essentially.

And so, with money from the Joseph P. Kennedy, Sr., Foundation, they airlifted 280 Africans to different universities. Barack Obama, Senior, went to the University of Hawaii. This was all organized by Tom Mboya (**Slide 2**), who was willing to cooperate with the CIA to some extent. You had some pan-African Congresses in 1958 (**Slide 3**), and there was a concern about Soviet intermingling with these nations at these conferences,—and so the CIA selected Mboya as our man in Kenya. They were concerned about Prime Minister Kwame Nkrumah of Ghana, later the great personal friend of President John Kennedy. But the Allen Dulles faction of the CIA hated Nkrumah.

So, Obama's father was friends with Mboya. He helped Mboya to form one of the Kenyan political parties.

So, Mboya picked Obama senior and other people who were part of his political party, to go to American universities. Mboya was assassinated in 1969. Obama's father testified at the trial of the assassin.

Slide—Here's the Hands Off Africa—Africa Must be Free! (**Slide 4**) This was the conference where the CIA tried to recruit Mboya. This was the all-African People's Conference in Tunisia in 1959. And the CIA noticed that serious friction developed between Nkrumah and Mboya, and they also stated in the report that Mboya was cooperating effectively to check the extemists. He was described in another CIA memorandum, as an "able, dynamic chairman, viewed as an opponent to the Sino-Soviet support of Nkrumah."

Nkrumah was the Prime Minister and then the President of Ghana, and he was overthrown in 1966 when he was away. (**Slide 5**) That's him, that's a picture of him with President Kennedy in earlier days. Mboya was assassinated. Obama's father died in—he was in a car crash, I think, in 1982, and other friends of Obama senior and Mboya were also assassinated. Jomo Kenyatta, who was the President of Kenya, dismissed all of his cabinet members who belonged to this party, after this string of murders, in 1975.

Slide (**Slide 6**)—That's Obama's mom. This is him in Hawaii. It doesn't look like Obama's mom, but it looks like he's talking to her about very interesting things.

Slide 8

Slide 9

Slide 10

Enter the Indonesian Colonel

(**Slide 7**) Obama's stepfather. So, Obama has no dad. Obama senior leaves, and his mom meets Lolo Soetoro, who goes to the University of Hawaii from Indonesia, to get an education. And they met in 1965 at the University of Hawaii's East-West center. They get married in '65 (**Slide 8**), and then the same year, he leaves. He has to go back to Indonesia. He's been summoned back to participate in the overthrow of Sukarno, which was an armed coup against Sukarno.

(**Slide 9** This is the general who led the coup, Suharto. This was a bloody coup that involved massacres of hundreds of thousands of people who were the enemy, and Obama's step-father, Lolo Soetoro, was an army colonel, one of the main army advisers to Suharto, and helped him in this post-coup period of purging the "communist enemy."

So he left Obama and his mom three months before the coup, and then, a year later, Obama and his mom go to live with him in Indonesia. It was the same year that the CIA overthrew Nkrumah in Ghana, too. This was in 1966.

So, this coup happens. General Suharto is leading Indonesia now. Indonesia realigns its economy and starts getting assistance from the IMF. They start getting monetary assistance. And there's still resistance in parts of Java, in the eastern and central parts of Java, but Obama's mom would "take care of that," which is what I'm going to get into now.

Ann Gets a Job

This is kind of like the Great Mother in the Odyssey. (**Slide 10**)] This is Barack Obama's mother talking with—it looks like a CIA agent. [laughter] This happens to be in Indonesia.

So, in 1967, a year after this bloody coup in Indonesia, she takes Obama to go live with Lolo Soetoro. Obama's raised by Lolo Soetoro's transvestite housekeeper when he's away massacring the Chinese and the communist Indonesians. And Obama's mom is really interesting. I don't know how to describe it really. She's basically,—it's weird. After I describe it, it'll make sense to you, what it is. Basically she was a CIA agent during this period, which was the period of the war in Indo-China. Keep in mind that the war in Vietnam is going on during all of this.

She's often-times portrayed as like a hippy lib-

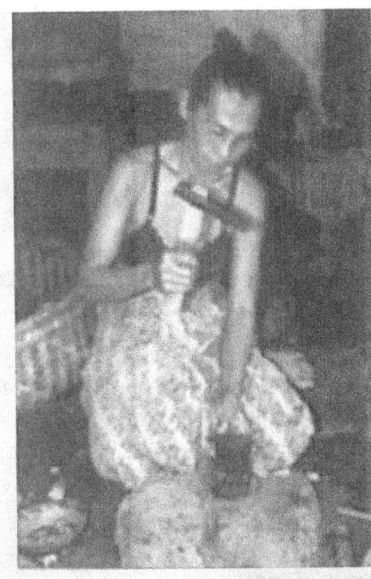

Slide 11

Slide 12

Slide 13

eral,—but she wasn't in Indonesia protesting the war; she was actually profiling,—she was trained to profile the villagers throughout Indonesia, to sort of mark them as "loyal" or "disloyal," and then her husband would go and get rid of them. I think he studied geography at the University of Hawaii, so he had a reason to go there to study maps and what-not.

What she did, though, is, she worked for the U.S. Agency for International Development (USAID), in Jakarta, and she taught English to people at the American embassy there. And she also had a lot of activity throughout Southeast Asia: like in South Vietnam, Thailand, Laos. She travelled all over: Bangladesh, Pakistan, India. She also, throughout her career, she worked for the Ford Foundation, the World Bank, the Asian Development Bank, as well as USAID. And she started out teaching English to CIA agents, and people who were being recruited to become CIA agents from Indonesia. And then, she got involved in micro-loans.

And this was said as kind of like a praise, or defense, of her: She was giving micro-loans. But you can't think of a more evil thing to do, than give someone a micro-loan.

She was working for Peter Geithner, who was Timothy Geithner's father. He allotted the money, and she would profile,—because she also studied anthropology, so she would go and profile these people, who would get loans.

These are from her scrapbook.

Question: Was Peter Geithner also a CIA agent? Yes.

There she is with this old Indonesian lady, in her sandals and sunglasses. Oh look: Doesn't she look happy, actually?

(**Slide 11**) This is what she helped to finance, with these micro-loans,—was slave labor production.

(**Slide 12**) There she is, holding a little duck or chicken. And there's a basket,—maybe that was made by a woman for .05 cents.

(**Slide 13**) Here's other things that her micro-loans helped to support. This man being able to make,—who knows what?—no shoes, but he's got a job.

(**Slide 14**) Here's some more benefactors of the micro-loans. And you really don't know what they're making, because it might have something to

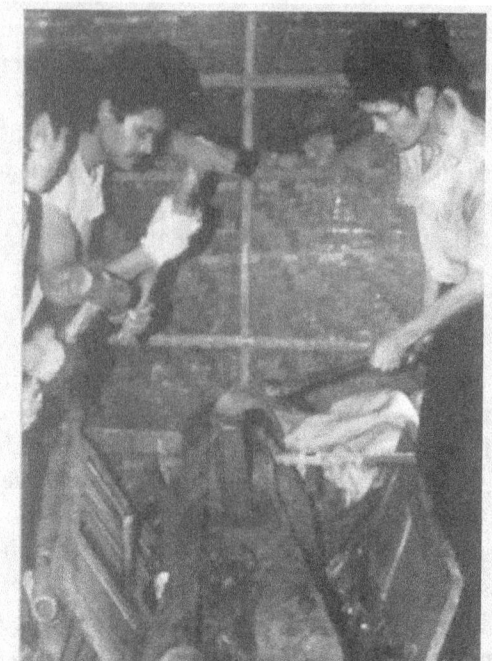

Slide 14

Slide 15

Slide 16

do with the Vietnam war.

(**Slide 15:**)She's always smiling.

(**Slide 16:**)You don't want to wear a shirt. It gets hot in these parts.

(**Slide 17**) Oh, And there's her desk.

AID, CIA: Profiling the Enemy

The company she worked for was the U.S. Agency for International Development (USAID). This was the CIA. They supplied rice to the Laotian army, and the Laotian army resold it to the North Vietnamese,—and when this came out, they said, "Should we be doing this? Should we be supporting the enemy? They said, "No, no, no, it's okay, because it's keeping them from,—we're basically buying off the Laotians. They're not going to ally with the communists, even though they're supplying the North Vietnamese." It was with strings attached. It was to get them to support the war against the communists in Southeast Asia.

Other programs the USAID conducted were for injured civilians. Lots of money was allotted for injured civilians, which was diverted for military purposes. In 1971, USAID and the CIA were accused of losing $1.7 billion, somehow, in South Vietnam. USAID money was directed to the CIA's proprietary airline in Southeast Asia,—Air America,—and in Thailand, USAID funds for an "accelerated rural development program," were actually masking CIA anti-communist counterinsurgency operations.

In 1971, in Pakistan, where Obama's mom also worked, funds from the USAID were used for East Pakistan's military fortifications on the border with India, in the months before the outbreak of war with India. In 1972, USAID funneled money to the Southern part, only, of North Yemen, to aid North Yemen's forces against the government of South Yemen.

USAID worked on all these projects with the Asia Foundation, which financed the guesthouse at the University of Hawaii, where Barack Obama's father stayed when he was airlifted there by the CIA.

As you start to see who she was, and what she was doing: this is all one thing, the same thing,—this is the key apparatus that killed Kennedy, that organized the war,—and she was

Slide 17

Slide 18

Slide 19

employed by these people.

Three years before she went to Southeast Asia, Indonesia, to give micro-loans, and to teach people English—there was a CIA project which was based on using anthropologists in the field to get intelligence, and they were sent all over. So, basically their education in anthropology was to support the missions of the CIA,—kind of a Margaret Mead-type, in that sense. (**Slide 18**)

I don't have pictures of her, but Obama's grandmother was the first female vice-president of the Bank of Hawaii, which various CIA front-entities used for their escrow accounts. And what Obama's grandmother, Madeleine Dunham, handled, was making the CIA payments to various rulers,—like Ferdinand Marcos in the Philippines, Nguyen Van Thieu in South Vietnam, as well as Suharto in Indonesia. The bank also helped to money-launder funds to support espionage in Japan, to arm the Afghan mujahideen, and also to provide weapons to Taiwan.

(**Slide 19**) And then there's a picture of Obama's father,—this one's weird, too. This is Obama's father off the plane from Kenya, with Obama's grandfather, Stanley Dunham,—which is just weird, because Obama's mom's dad met her husband before she did,—before she met him at school in the Russian language class.

Question: This is in Kenya?

This is in Hawaii. He just got off the plane with this lei that they give you.

Wayne Madsen gets into the strong possibility that he was also a CIA agent in Beirut, Lebanon in the 50s, doing CIA work. In other words, that he wasn't a furniture salesman who travelled to all the CIA hotspots.

Truth is stranger than fiction, as Mark Twain said.

Pamela Churchill Harriman Was Not Amused

It was a lovely spring day in Georgetown in June 1982. Democratic Party doyenne Pamela Harriman was hosting a garden party fundraiser for her wing of the party. Strangely, guests were entering the garden with programs, printed on bright golden paper. She had ordered no such programs. Even stranger was the look on their faces as they read the program.—Susan Kokinda

As a contributor to

Democrats for the '80s

You Are Invited to A

Reception

commemorating the

GOLDEN   ANNIVERSARY

of the

1932 Eugenics Conference

The conference sponsored by and dedicated to

Mary Harriman
(the late mother of Governor Harriman)

Proceeds from the affair
will go to the
Fund to Endow a Nobel Prize in
Race Science

Anglo-Saxons only
need RSVP

Music by the Cliveden Set
Catering by Aryan Freres

Front Cover

A Golden Anniversary

The Harriman family has been active in many causes. On Feb. 10, 1927, the *New York Times* carried an article entitled, "Harriman Returns from Tour Abroad, Saw Mussolini in Rome." The article quotes the foresightful Averell Harriman directly on how he was "very much impressed" with the economic development of Italy under Mussolini.

But this was merely a precursor of things to come, and Americans would be remiss if they did not take pause to commemorate the 50th Anniversary of one particular project of Mrs. Mary Harriman, the late mother of Averell. The 1932 Eugenics Conference, held at New York's Museum of Natural History—sponsored by, attended by, and ultimately dedicated to Mrs. Mary Harriman—had truly world-shattering effects.

At the pinnacle of its accomplishments was the *unanimous* election of Alfred Plotz, of the German Society for Racial Hygiene, as President of the International Eugenics Society. Another conference attendee, Ernst Rudin (the President of the German Society for Racial Hygiene), spoke of Plotz eight years later in a 1940 obituary: "It is tragic that Plotz did not live to see the solution to the problem of understanding and cooperation amongst the Nordic races, when he had believed so ardently in the purposeful leadership of Adolf Hitler and his holy national and international racial hygienic mission."

Rudin, himself, would later gain

far-reaching attention as:

- The author of the Nazi law "For the Protection of German Blood and German Honor" which declared Jews to be non-citizens;
- The forced sterilization programs of "mental defectives";
- The T-4 program, which trained the operators of the concentration camps.

Your host and hostess tonight might agree that there are lessons for our time in the keynote address, delivered by Henry Fairfield Osborne, director of the Museum of Natural History and nephew of J.P. Morgan. Mr. Osborne forcefully argued that "overpopulation and unemployment are twin sisters.... The unemployed are naturally the less competent. In nature, they would disappear but in civilization we are keeping them in the community in the hope that in better days they may all find employment. This is only another instance of humane civilization going directly against the order of nature and encouraging the survival of the unfittest. The slogan, "Not More, But Better, Americans" should have its counterpart in every country in the world in which the rising spirit of nationalism and of an entirely natural and reasonable pride should be accomplished by the consciousness that the quality rather than quantity is the essential element of progress in every country and in every race."

Another attendee and associate of the Harrimans, the Teddy Roosevelt family, and Osborne was Madison Grant, the head of the Immigration Restriction League. Grant wrote: "In the city of New York and elsewhere in the United States there is a native American aristocracy resting upon layer after layer of immigrants of lower races.... *It has taken us 50 years to learn that speaking English, wearing good clothes and going to school and church does not transform a Negro into a white man.* And we will have similar experiences with Polish Jews, whose dwarf stature and peculiar mentality are being engrafted upon the stock of the nation.

Nor should we forget Dr. Charles Davenport, the head of the Harriman-funded Records Office, who asked, "Can we by eugenics studies produce supermen? Progress will come slowly, but it will come." Dr. Davenport was an afficianado of human breeding techniques.

The National Democratic Policy Committee, which issued this flyer, was the predecessor organization of LaRouchePAC.

```
           The Golden Jubilee will

             culminate in the

               PRESENTATION

                  of the

   ERNST RUDIN QUALITY OF LIFE AWARD

                    to

            Charles B. Manatt
                 Chairman
       Democratic National Committee


        Presenting the Award will be

                 Governor
         Jerry "Il Douche" Brown


     THE RUDIN AWARD is sponsored by:

     Resources for the Few
     The 2nd Century Fund
     The Fund for an Anglo-Saxon Majority
```

```
The current policies of the Harrimans     Your presence is
and their co-thinkers continue in the      urgently requested
tradition of the 1932 Eugenics Con-
ference.  For those of you who agree       Time: 1982
that White Anglo-Saxon racism has          Place: Nuremburg
no place in America, call the NDPC.

Authorized and paid for by the
NATIONAL DEMOCRATIC POLICY COMMITTEE
(as a public service of its
"Knew or Should Have Known" division)
          223-5614
```

Back Cover

Obama *Is* the Detonator for World War

by Jeffrey Steinberg

April 27—Developments over the past ten days provide a devastating reminder that, as long as Barack Obama remains in office as President, the world stands on the edge of general war, a war that could quickly become a war of thermonuclear extinction.

A series of warnings and alarming events indicate how close the "unsurvivable" is coming:

• the solemn warning jointly written by high-ranking retired American and Russian generals, "How To Avoid a Nuclear War," published April 19 by the *New York Times*;

• the warnings that nuclear war is threatening, issued by the top Russian military officials at the Moscow Security Conference;

• the changes being made by the U.S. Joint Strike Command which blur the distinction between nuclear and conventional weapon use across all platforms of the Command;

• Obama's full military backing for a new war launched by Saudi Arabia against Yemen, which is intended to stage a general war confrontation against Iran;

• the start of U.S. military training for Ukraine forces that incorporate openly Nazi anti-Russian units.

The British Going Wild

The issue is not Obama per se. He is a degenerate patsy of the British Empire and allied Wall Street forces, which are currently being driven mad by the reality that their trans-Atlantic financial system is doomed, and that an alternative paradigm, centered in the China/Russia-led emerging BRICS system, is coming into being. The forces which have owned Obama, since they launched his political career decades ago, are ready to start World War III, rather than surrender their power.

Lyndon LaRouche warned on April 21 that "we are on the verge of virtual extinction, as the result of chain-reaction effects of this situation." The refusal of the British and Wall Street to surrender their failing grip on power will drive them, in desperation, to have Obama launch World War III. "This is the first threat of human extinction in modern history," LaRouche concluded.

He further observed, that the mere fact that Obama has not yet been removed from office, is the clearest warning that leading American circles, and the American people as a whole, no longer possess the temperament to stop this disaster from occurring. Remove Obama from the Presidency, and the danger is removed. The British will remain hysterical over the imminent demise of their empire, but they will be rendered powerless to act. The bankruptcy of the trans-Atlantic system means the death of the British Empire.

Russian vitality has returned, and China is emerging as a friendly, but dominant force in Asia, promoting a policy of "win-win" cooperation among all of the nations of the region and across Eurasia. This alone is driving the British wild.

It is vital to comprehend these *motives* behind the war danger. The day-by-day events are merely markers of that process—warning signs along the road to potential doom.

The Threat of Extinction

The Fourth Moscow International Security Conference on April 18-19 made clear that Russian leaders clearly understand the imminent danger of thermonuclear war. It was the dominant theme of the major conference presentations by Russia's Defense Minister Sergei Shoigu, Foreign Minister Sergei Lavrov, and Chief of the General Staff Valery Gerasimov. The audience and speakers list included the ministers of defense of all of key Eurasian nations: China, India, Iran, Pakistan, North Korea, Greece, Iran, Indonesia, Mongolia, Serbia, and Belarus, plus South Africa.

Lavrov made clear in his remarks that the U.S. and NATO deployment of the anti-ballistic missile systems to areas bordering on Russia constitutes a threat of a first-strike attack on Russia. President Obama had claimed that the ABM systems were directed at Iran, not at Russia,

DOD/D. Myles Cullen

Retired generals James Cartwright (U.S., left) and Vladimir Dvorkin (Russia) issued a joint appeal to stop the drive toward nuclear war.

and that the deployment would be re-assessed if a P5+1 deal on Iran's nuclear program were reached. Now that such a deal is within reach, Obama has refused to scale back or cancel the ABM deployments, which will place vital components of the missile defense shield in Romania and Poland, near Russia's borders.

In an unprecedented recognition of the threat of nuclear armageddon, two leading retired generals—from the United States and Russia—produced a joint op-ed in the *New York Times* of April 19, headlined "How To Avert a Nuclear War." Gen. James E. Cartwright (USMC-ret.), former Vice Chairman of the Joint Chiefs of Staff and Commander of the U.S. Strategic Command; and Gen. Vladimir Dvorkin (ret.), former head of the research institute for Russia's Strategic Rocket Forces, warned that the breakdown of communications between Washington and Moscow, since the Ukraine coup of February 2014, has increased the risk of thermonuclear war.

More Provocations for Mass Kill

The Obama Administration is taking other provocative actions that illustrate this point. The U.S. is expanding and radically altering its Global Strike Command, by reintegrating B-1 long-range bombers, to incorporate both conventional weapons and strategic nuclear weapons. In addition, the Administration is developing a new generation of tactical nuclear weapons, to be forward based in Europe and deployable on long-range stealth bombers and drones, armed with cruise missiles.

These two actions blur the lines between nuclear and conventional warfare, greatly increasing the prospects of

the use of nuclear weapons in Eurasia. They corrrespond to plans for a first strike on Russia, using a combination of conventional, nuclear, and missile defense capabilities to survive a nuclear war. While this is the greatest folly imaginable, it is precisely what is behind the plans.

While taking these steps towards potential thermonuclear confrontation in the heart of Eurasia, the British and Obama are simultaneously pursuing permanent population wars in the Persian Gulf and elsewhere.

The situation in the Persian Gulf, where the same Saudi forces that ran the 9/11 attacks against the United States—attacks that have been covered up by two successive Presidents, Bush and Obama—are engaging in a population war against neighbor Yemen, claiming that Houthi rebels there are surrogates for Iran. This is another flashpoint for imminent war.

When the P5+1 breakthrough was announced at the beginning of the month in Switzerland, LaRouche warned that the agreement would be a trigger for war—unless the Saudis were smashed. Instead, Obama joined forces with the Saudis in the bombing campaign against Yemen, over the strong objections of the U.S. Joint Chiefs of Staff and the Central Command.

As the Gulf of Aden filled with Saudi and American warships, in the past week, including the aircraft carrier *USS Theodore Roosevelt*, and Obama threatened actions against Iranian commercial vessels en route to Yemen, intense pressure from the U.S. military and other circles led the Saudis to announce a halt to their bombing campaign late on April 21. Earlier in the day, King Salman had put the Saudi National Guard on alert for possible ground operations across the border into Yemen. The circumstances of the last-moment freeze in operations are still to be sorted out, but the fact remains that the region was headed towards a "Gulf of Tonkin" type provocation for war, that was only halted at the last moment—and has already been resumed on a limited scale.

The doom of civilization is not inevitable. But it is virtually a certainty unless Obama is removed from office. He is the detonator for world war, and his prompt removal is the only legitimate war-prevention option at this late date.

Two Bandung Conferences: Preventing Thermonuclear War

by Mike Billington

April 24—Representatives from 92 African and Asian nations gathered this April 22-23 in Jakarta and Bandung, Indonesia, to celebrate the 60th anniversary of the Asian-African Summit held in Bandung in April 1955. What is immediately apparent, and striking, from reading and comparing the speeches presented this last week, and those given 60 years ago at the original Bandung Conference, is that in both cases, the leaders of the nations of Asia and Africa were (are) confronting the threat of thermonuclear war emanating from the dominant powers of the "West." In both cases, these leaders recognized that it was a primary responsibility of the nations of the formerly colonized world, to counter the war-mongering and geopolitics of the advanced sector leaders, with a moral outlook toward the future, based on the common aims of mankind.

The primary difference between 1955 and 2015, is that the former colonial nations, which were economically and strategically weak after achieving independence, are now increasingly prosperous, and, under the leadership of the BRICS nations, capable of challenging the Western policies of war and austerity with one of Peace through Development for the world as a whole.

Looking especially at the speeches in Bandung by Chinese President Xi Jinping on April 22, 2015, and by Indonesian President (and the father of Indonesian independence) Sukarno in 1955, it is evident that the new paradigm for peace and development being led today by the BRICS, their New Development Bank, the Chinese-initiated Asia Infrastructure Investment Bank, and through China's Silk Road initiatives, represents the fulfillment of the Spirit of Bandung.

The Spirit of Bandung

The Spirit of Bandung, which became the driving inspiration for the Non-Aligned Movement, was organized primarily by Indonesian President Sukarno and Indian Prime Minister Jawaharlal Nehru, and brought together 25 national leaders from Asia, Africa, and the Mideast. It was the first meeting of former colonial nations without the presence of their former colonial masters. A major focus of the conference was mitigating the severe threat of war between the United States and China, and China's then-Foreign Minister Zhou Enlai played a leading role there. In 1954, Zhou, India's Nehru, and Burma's Ne Win had jointly adopted "The Five Principles of Peaceful Coexistence," which were subsequently adopted by the Bandung conference. They were based on mutual respect for sovereignty, territorial integrity, non-interference in internal affairs, cooperation for mutual benefit, and peaceful coexistence.

President Sukarno's speech opening the 1955 Bandung Conference (see following article) captured both the danger of a new thermonuclear world war, and the moral responsibility of the African and Asian nations—which had won their independence through bloody wars, as in Indonesia, or by equally bloody violent and non-violent resistance, as in India—to take actions to prevent that war, and to create a world based on harmony and development.

Sukarno warned: "Our unhappy world is torn and tortured, and the peoples of all countries walk in fear, lest, through no fault of theirs, the dogs of war are unchained once again." He noted that in the age of thermonuclear weapons, civilization itself was at risk.

He added: "Perhaps now more than at any other moment in the history of the world, society, government, and statesmanship need to be based upon the highest code of morality and ethics. And in political terms, what is the highest code of morality? It is the subordination of everything to the well-being of mankind."

He praised the gathered leaders for the successful liberation of their countries from colonialism, while also warning that "colonialism also has its modern dress, in the form of economic control, intellectual control, and actual physical control by a small but alien community within a nation."

London and Dulles

Such truthful talk from colonial "wogs" was not appreciated in London, nor by London's assets in the United States—and most emphatically not by Secretary of State John Foster Dulles and his brother, CIA chief Allen Dulles. Sukarno was marked for elimination.[1]

But the primary target of that planned elimination was China. John Foster Dulles was itching for a war with Maoist China, and was already fuming that President Eisenhower had rejected his advice to use nuclear weapons to aid the French in their losing colonial war against the Vietnamese. He ostentatiously refused to shake the outstretched hand of Zhou Enlai at the 1954 Geneva Peace Conference (which addressed both the Korean and the Vietnamese wars).

Xinhua/Li Xueren

Chinese President Xi Jinping and Indonesian President Joko Widodo lead a march in Bandung, April 24, 2015.

The 1955 defeat of the French by the Vietnamese at Dienbienphu, together with the successful Asia-Africa Conference at Bandung, was the last straw for the Dulles boys and their Wall Street/City of London sponsors. A three part strategy was devised and implemented:

1. Bring down Sukarno in a manner that would serve as an ugly example to other former colonial nations that might reject what Sukarno had identified as neo-colonial status;

2. Bring about a U.S. war in Vietnam, to complete the job the French had failed to accomplish; and

3. Encircle China militarily and economically (as Obama is doing today) in such a way as to either provoke a war (with U.S. use of nuclear weapons), or to so isolate China that it collapsed internally.

All these plans were successfully implemented, resulting in six decades of tragedy for mankind.

The history of the U.S. self-destructive and genocidal war against Vietnam is well-documented. Here we need only add that the triggers for unleashing that bestiality were the assassinations of President John F. Kennedy and of Vietnamese President Ngo Dinh Diem. Kennedy had already decided that he would not deploy troops into the Vietnamese civil war, and that he would move to establish diplomatic ties with China in his second term. Diem had made clear that he would rather strike a deal with the Viet Cong and the North Vietnamese, than allow the United States to take over the battle with the insurgents, and plunge his country back into colonial warfare.

The assassination of Diem and his brother Ngo Dinh Nhu was accomplished on Nov. 2, 1963, on the orders of Ambassadors W. Averell Harriman and Henry Cabot Lodge, behind the back of President Kennedy. Kennedy was eliminated three weeks later on Nov. 22, assassinated by the British. London and Wall Street had their new colonial war in Vietnam within a few short months.

---

1. For a full exposition on the disastrous phase shift in history directed by the British and their agents between 1963 and 1966, see "When America Let Britain Run, and Ruin, U.S. Asia Policy" in *EIR*, Sept. 7, 2001.

The Indonesia Bloodbath

In Indonesia, the CIA instigated revolts in the late 1950s against Sukarno, utilizing dissident military factions, directly funded, armed, and trained by the CIA. The United States then used air power by unmarked bombers from the U.S. base at Clark Airfield in the Philippines to back up the dissidents. But these failed to unseat the wildly popular Sukarno. Dulles and his fellow criminals in London and Australia then blamed an obscure coup attempt in 1965 on the Indonesian Communist Party (PKI), and on Sukarno himself.

The targeting of the PKI had two strategic purposes. First, the party was part of the broad base of support for Sukarno's Indonesia National Party, which had established cooperation between nationalists, communists, and religious institutions. Second, the PKI was the world's largest communist movement outside of China, and, like the Sukarno government itself, had excellent relations with the Chinese government. To wipe it out would send a strong message to Beijing.

What followed was one of the greatest genocides of the 20th Century, as approximately half a million people (the exact number will never be known) were slaughtered, mostly by mobs of radical Islamists wielding machetes. These mobs were openly backed by the U.S., British and Australian Embassies. While the slaughter was aimed at members of the PKI, any supporter of Sukarno was conveniently labeled a communist, and therefore targeted for killing.

Cables released years later from the western embassies, showed their direct support for the slaughter. The U.S. Embassy provided a list of as many as 5,000 "communists" in villages where CIA operatives were active, marking them for death. There was virtually no resistance from the peaceful Sukarno supporters.

Inside China, the military threat represented by the launching of full-scale U.S. war on its border in Vietnam, together with the slaughter of its political allies in Indonesia, led to the defeat of the Zhou Enlai faction within Mao Zedong's leadership circle. Zhou's global effort to establish peaceful relations with all countries, East and West, based on the Five Principles of Peaceful Coexistence, had been absolutely rejected by the Wall

The Bandung conference of 1955 was the first meeting of former colonial nations without the presence of their former colonial masters.

Street/British forces which had taken control in Washington, and was therefore discarded. Mao then unleashed the ten-year nightmare known as the Great Proletarian Cultural Revolution, a self-destructive attack on science, Classical Confucian culture, and on life itself.

The British imperialists, and their Washington cohorts, were pleased.

Restoring the Spirit of Bandung

The 2015 Anniversary Bandung Conference came at a time when the world is facing the greatest threat of global thermonuclear war in modern history—a threat far greater than at the peak of the Cold War, when the first Bandung Conference took place. The Western world—the former colonial powers—are undergoing a general economic breakdown crisis. At the same time, they see their former colonies, united under the leadership of the BRICS nations, now economically strong enough to resist the economic dictates of austerity and forced backwardness, from their former masters.

The BRICS global dynamic is creating a new paradigm based on a commitment to building infrastructure projects spanning Asia, Africa, and Ibero-America, and to forging what Chinese President Xi Jinping calls "win-win" cooperation. The BRICS countries have the support of nearly all the nations of Asia, Africa, and Ibero-America, and, united in this way, are also capable of defeating the evil "color revolution" campaigns, the modern form of subversion and destruction of sovereign nations.

It is this threat to the power of the London and New York banking oligarchs, which is creating the new thrust toward global war. The financial oligarchy, Obama firmly in tow, would rather go to war than relinquish their power over the world.

This issue was implicitly taken up in the opening speech by the newly elected Indonesian President Joko Widodo: "The idea that the world's economic problems can be solved only through the World Bank, IMF, and ADB is obsolete and must be abandoned. I am of the opinion that the fate of the global economy should not only be left to those three financial institutions. It is imperative that we build a new international economic order that is open to new emerging economic powers." He called on the Asian and African nations to push for reform of the United Nations, describing it as powerless to resolve problems of global imbalances and injustices, pointing to the Palestinian conflict in particular.

President Widodo, known as Jokowi, is a member of the Indonesian Democratic Party-Struggle (PDI-P), a party headed by former President Megawati Sukarnoputri, the daughter of Sukarno!

In Chinese President Xi's speech to the conference, he expressed agreement with Jokowi's call for a new world economic order. Praising the Spirit of Bandung which "galvanized a movement of national liberation throughout the world," he said in his speech: "It is important to prod developed countries to earnestly deliver on their commitments, and step up their support for developing countries with no political strings attached." He said that by the end of the year, China would extend zero-tariff treatment to 97% of taxable goods coming from all the least-developed countries that have diplomatic ties with China.

President Xi pointed to the AIIB and the "One Road, One Belt" Silk Road policies, as being dedicated to connectivity and development throughout Asia and Africa and beyond. "We are different among ourselves, and together we face the challenges ahead," Xi said. "However, we have learned to see things in common. We believe that if you want to go fast, go alone, but if you want to go far, go together—and we know that together we are strong. In April 2015, history awaits a new miracle of Asia and Africa at the Bandung Conference."

mobeir@aol.com

President Sukarno at the Bandung Conference, 1955

The following is excerpted from Indonesian President Sukarno's <u>speech</u> to the 1955 Bandung Conference.

Indonesian President Sukarno at Bandung in 1955.

Our unhappy world is torn and tortured, and the peoples of all countries walk in fear lest, through no fault of theirs, the dogs of war are unchained once again.

Yes, there has indeed been a *"Sturm über Asien"* [Storm over Asia]—and over Africa too. The last few years have seen enormous changes. Nations, states, have awoken from a sleep of centuries. The passive peoples have gone, the outward tranquility has made place for struggle and activity. Irresistible forces have swept the two continents. The mental, spiritual and political face of the whole world has been changed, and the process is still not complete....

Perhaps now more than at any other moment in the history of the world, society, government and statesmanship need to be based upon the highest code of morality and ethics. And in political terms, what is the highest code of morality? It is the subordination of everything to the well-being of mankind.

But today we are faced with a situation where the well-being of mankind is not always the primary consideration. Many who are in places of high power, think, rather, of controlling the world.

Yes, we are living in a world of fear. The life of man today is corroded and made bitter by fear. Fear of the future, fear of the hydrogen bomb, fear of ideologies. Perhaps this fear is a greater danger than the danger itself, because it is fear which drives men to act foolishly, to act thoughtlessly, to act dangerously. In your deliberations, Sisters and Brothers, I beg of you, do not be guided by these fears, because fear is an acid which etches man's actions into curious patterns. Be guided by hopes and determination, be guided by ideals, and, yes, be guided by dreams!...

The battle against colonialism has been a long one, and do you know that today is a famous anniversary in that battle? On the eighteenth day of April, 1775, just one hundred and eighty years ago, Paul Revere rode at midnight through the New England countryside, warning of the approach of British troops and of the opening of the American War of Independence, the first successful anti-colonial war in history. About this midnight ride the poet Longfellow wrote:

"A cry of defiance and not of fear,
"A voice in the darkness, a knock at the door,
"And a word that shall echo for evermore."

Yes, it shall echo for evermore, just as the other anti-colonial words which gave us comfort and reassurance during the darkest days of our struggle shall echo for evermore. But remember, that battle which began 180 years ago is not yet completely won, and it will not have been completely won, until we can survey this our own world, and can say that colonialism is dead....

War would not only mean a threat to our independence: it may mean the end of civilisation and even of human life. There is a force loose in the world whose potentiality for evil no man truly knows. Even in practice and rehearsal for war. the effects may well be building up into something of unknown horror.

What can we do? We can do much! We can inject the voice of reason into world affairs. We can mobilise all the spiritual, all the moral, all the political strength of Asia and Africa on the side of peace. Yes, we! We, the peoples of Asia and Africa, 1,400,000,000 strong, far more than half the human population of the world,—we can mobilise what I have called the Moral Violence of Nations in favour of peace. We can demonstrate to the minority of the world which lives on the other continents, that we, the majority, are for peace, not for war,— and that whatever strength we have will always be thrown onto the side of peace

Our task is first to seek an understanding of each other, and out of that understanding will come a greater appreciation of each other, and out of that appreciation will come collective action. Bear in mind the words of one of Asia's greatest sons [Sun Yat-sen—ed.]: "To speak is easy. To act is hard. To understand is hardest. Once one understands, action is easy."

II. The Nature and Destiny of Man

The New Presidency

by Matthew Ogden

Matthew Ogden delivered the following introductory remarks to the LaRouchePAC weekly webcast of April 24, 2015.

Good evening.... I'm joined here in the studio by both Benjamin Deniston and Jason Ross from the LaRouchePAC Scientific "Basement" Team.

This broadcast is intended to serve as a sort of prelude to an event which is happening tomorrow, a live town hall meeting which will be simulcast from three locations—New York City, California, and Texas—and will be addressed by Kesha Rogers and Michael Steger—both members of the LaRouchePAC Policy Committee—as well as Ben Deniston.

If you've been joining us over the last few weeks, you'll know that the LaRouchePAC has set a new standard of leadership with the presentations that Ben Deniston has given, both on these broadcasts and also elsewhere. Our job here tonight, is to draw out the implications of what Ben has presented from the standpoint of this question: What is the human species? What is our mission in the Solar System? And, what must be done to ensure that mankind fulfills this mission?

Mr. LaRouche emphasized earlier today that the problem that we face is that very few people in positions of leadership rise to that standard—the standard which was set by the presentations that Ben Deniston has given. You do have a very small but qualified number of leaders in areas of this planet such as the government of China, and related countries such as the constituent countries among the BRICS [Brazil, Russia, India, China, South Africa], who *do* rise to that level of responsible leadership.

However, here in the United States, we confront what you could call an epidemic of stupidity and pragmatism. You have the press, the mass media, the members of Congress, elected officials generally, and the American public in general, who have *no* efficient understanding of the gravity and the profundity of the challenges which confront mankind. They have no *real* insight into reality, and they instead substitute a narrative which they wish to be overheard supporting, and feel comfortable being overheard supporting, but which has no basis in provable scientific fact. They adopt slogans, they adopt positions on so-called political issues, some of which may even be the correct ones; but these opinions will tend to have no real merit in fact, because they're not formed from the standpoint of scientific competence and scientific principle.So, this is the significance of what you've heard presented by Ben Deniston over the past several weeks, which sets an entirely different standard.

Mankind's Role in the Solar System

Now, as Mr. LaRouche emphasized in our discussion with him earlier, what we need is an efficient apprehension of mankind's true role in the Solar System and beyond, and the commitment to use every means available to mankind to fulfill that. Or, said otherwise, we need people to begin acting like human beings, and not just higher apes. We need to ask the question: What is the natural destiny of mankind? What is the current *ability* of Man to achieve that destiny? What *were* the potential *future* ability of mankind to achieve that destiny, were mankind to begin acting according to his true identity? And what is *hindering* mankind from attaining that future?

And it's from this standpoint that you can confront the crisis that we face here at home as well as abroad. Yes, indeed, the United States has a crisis—a big one—typified by Barack Obama; typified by [California Gov.] Jerry Brown; but it is not only the United States. Mankind *as a whole* is in a

EIRNS/Stuart Lewis

LaRouche and Reagan talk during a debate held in New Hampshire during the 1980 Presidential campaign. As author of the Strategic Defense Initiative, LaRouche was brought into the Reagan Presidency to carry out back-channel negotiations on the SDI.

crisis, which is caused by the way that mankind in general tends to think, and the way that governments tend to make policy based on their *failure* to take into account the identity and the true mission of mankind. *This* must be the starting-point, and not some afterthought. We have to begin from the standpoint of what the nature and the destiny of mankind must be, and then proceed from there—not the other way around.

And, as Mr. LaRouche also emphasized in our discussion today: The work that Ben Deniston has done achieves this standard, and allows us to do just that. It allows us to at least begin to perceive that mankind has a future destiny which we have barely even begun to understand. And this is an insight which should define an entirely new view of mankind's view of mankind himself.

So, the responsibility of those who *do* have this quality of insight is to educate and to lead the rest of society, and allow our fellow citizens to climb *upwards* to *this* level, to *this* view of the understanding of themselves, and make them *more* intelligent—as opposed to attempting to stoop down to their level for the sake of popularity, and, in so doing, make *yourself less* intelligent.

So, Mr. LaRouche said, "Ask yourself this question: How many members of Congress understand this, the nature of the human being? How can they pretend to have the authority to legislate the affairs of mankind, if they have *no* understanding of what mankind even is?"

So, the problem that we face, is the tendency by members of Congress and other elected officials—even

the relatively better ones—to submit to stupidity and to compromise with incompetence. And this is what is killing us—literally! Just look at the current potential for widespread depopulation and drastic rises in the death rate caused by the water crisis now in California and the other Western states. Look at the thousands of refugees who are drowning and dying in the Mediterranean, who are fleeing from the utter chaos which has been created as a *direct consequence* of Obama's illegal wars in Libya, against Syria, and the surrounding areas of North Africa. Look at the installation of an avowed Nazi government in Ukraine, and the looming threat of a thermonuclear war against Russia—but not only Russia, also not to mention China and elsewhere.

These are the consequences of the willingness to accept the general stupidity of so-called ``politics'' today, and to compromise with *both* what the Obama Administration and the Bush-dominated Republican Party represent.

The LaRouche-Reagan SDI

So, we at LaRouchePAC fully intend to create a *new* Presidency. But it must be created from this standpoint: What is the true mission of mankind, and what responsibility must our nation have to play its part in a *positive* way in allowing mankind to achieve that mission?

And we intend to do this much in the way that Lyndon LaRouche himself played a critical role in organizing the policy of the incoming Presidency of Ronald Reagan in the years leading up to his election in 1980 around what became known as the SDI, the Strategic Defense Initiative, which was an expression of the highest potentials of the human mind to harness the power of new physical principles in order to change mankind's view of himself as a species, change our relationship with the Solar System, and, in so doing, change the destiny of the human species itself, preventing the self-extermination of mankind through a holocaust of thermonuclear war.

However, because of the poisonous influence of the Bush family inside the Reagan Administration, that potential victory was sabotaged and derailed, and we now find ourselves on the verge of a war potentially far, far greater in magnitude and in destructive capability than what we faced even at the time of Reagan's Presidency—which is a danger that I believe underscores the responsibility that we have here, even as a small handful of leaders this country, all that much more.

Man as a Galactic Force

by Benjamin Deniston

Benjamin Deniston of the LaRouchePAC Science Team gave this presentation to the weekly larouchepac.com webcast on April 24.

To continue the discussion that we've initiated, really the campaign on this "water" issue: Mr. LaRouche wanted this raised again tonight, and brought to a new level, a new perspective on what we're dealing with when we're talking about the "water" crisis. As we've discussed, there is a crisis. There's a crisis in California. There's a crisis in other Western states in the United States. There are water crises in many nations and many regions around the world.

I think it's important to state, outright, that there is a water crisis, and there isn't a water crisis. We have immediate situations where people are threatened, populations are threatened, food supplies are threatened, with a lack of water, immediately.

This is, perhaps, most stark in the United States in California, as we've discussed. But, there is a deeper issue that we want to get into. The fact that we have a lack of water in this location or that location isn't necessarily a "water crisis" per se. It's a cultural crisis. It's a crisis, as Mr. LaRouche was saying earlier today, in the lack of understanding by leading policymakers of the very nature of mankind, of what it means to be human. As Matthew [Ogden] referenced, Mr. LaRouche was saying earlier today that we have legislators who legislate for a species that they don't really understand.

Jerry Brown's 'Carrying Capacity'

Leading this type of idiocy, is [California Gov.] Jerry Brown. He has said this in his own words. That's useful, because you can just quote him, so you don't have to do much work. You just repeat what the guy said, and you get a clear expression of the problem. When push came to shove on this water issue, and there he was, as the responsible governor for the state facing an imminent crisis for a lack of water, his reply was: Well, the state really only used to have 300–400,000 people anyways. Now we have almost 40 million. So, we're obviously way beyond the capacity of the state.

This is the most idiotic thing! You could say that about any part of the entire world. You could say that about Europe. Europe, a couple hundred years ago, had a much lower population, it had a lower "carrying capacity." You could support fewer people in Europe on the same European territory 300-400 years ago. The whole world used to be able to support only a few million people, if you go back a few hundred thousand years.

Yes, that's a true statement. There used to be 300–400,000 people in California. But you could say that about any part of the world.

What you see in such statements, is a *profound* lack of understanding of the fundamental nature of mankind. There's no fixed "carrying capacity" for mankind. Yes, there used to be 300,000 people. Mankind changed his relationship to the environment! Mankind progressed. Mankind increased the potential relative population density. Mankind was able to wield an effect, and we

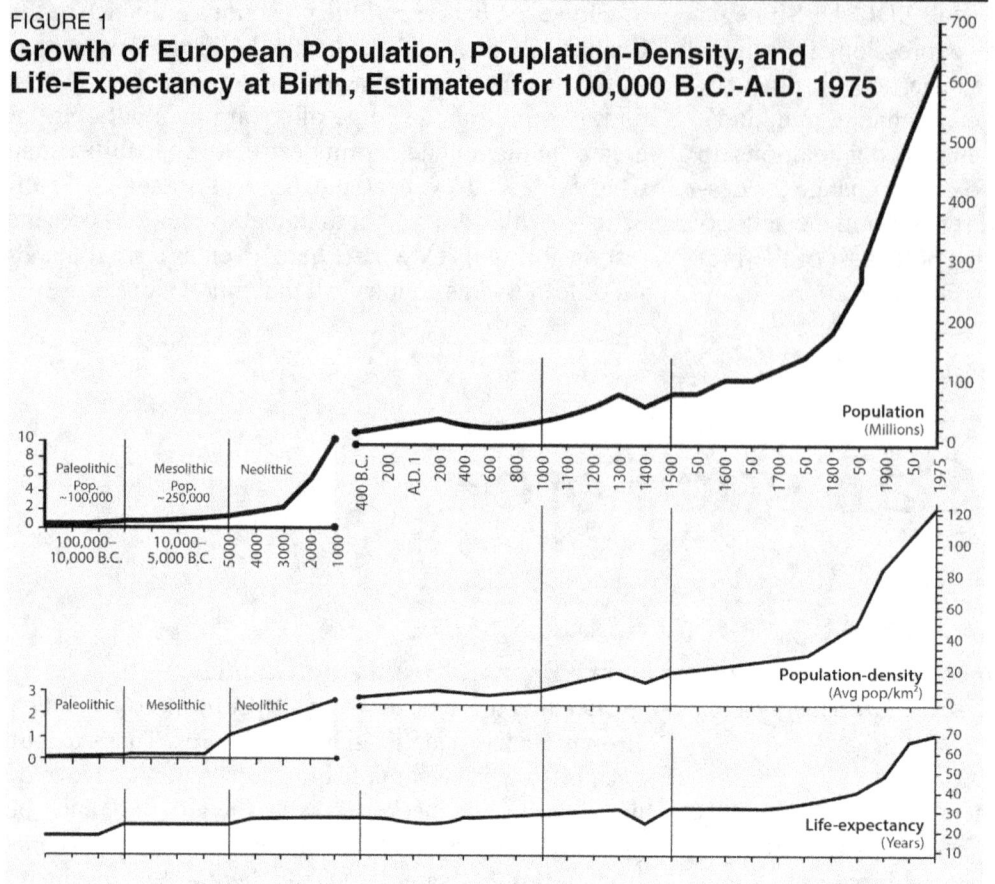

FIGURE 1
Growth of European Population, Pouplation-Density, and Life-Expectancy at Birth, Estimated for 100,000 B.C.-A.D. 1975

As opposed to all animal species, man has no fixed "carrying capacity." Over time, man has increased his overall population, life expectancy, and population-density, as shown here for the population of Europe since the Paleolithic period.

All charts are based on standard estimates compiled by existing schools of demography. None claim any more precision than the indicative; however, the scaling flattens out what might otherwise be locally, or even temporarily, significant variation, reducing all thereby to the set of changes which is significant, independent of the quality of estimate and scaling of the graps. Sources: For population and population-density, Colin McEvedy and Richard Jones, Atlas of World Population History; for life-expectancy, various studies in historical demography.

created, out of a desert, the most productive state in the entire country. That's typical of what mankind does, as real human nature. **(Figure 1)**

So, to cite the idea that the "carrying capacity" of the state used to be a small fraction of what it is now, and that somehow we should base our policy on that, is utterly insane. It's a lack of understanding, again, of the fundamental nature of the human species, of mankind.

Using that as a typical expression of the failed level of thinking that we're dealing with, what Mr. LaRouche said we want to get at today, is how do we approach this as *humans*, rather than as animals? Jerry Brown defined the "animal approach." That's his policy: depopulate, go back to a level where you only have a fraction of the population that there is now, because he has no understand-

ing of the true nature of mankind and human progress.

Water Is Not 'Finite'

But how do we address this as human beings? How do we, as a unique species on this planet, fundamentally different from animals, approach the situation around water, the water crisis?

Take a first look: You're dealing with water, what do you see? We see we have a global system. First, it's not a finite supply. We're not using up water supplies. You have a cyclical system that involves the whole planet. And what mankind has been able to do is manage those cycles, manage those systems, to make them more productive, to allow mankind to expand populations, develop deserts, develop arid regions, develop agriculture. And mankind has managed—not by drawing down some finite supply the way people talk about it today—but we've managed these cycles, these systems of water on the planet, to our needs to ensure we make the system able to support higher living standards of a growing population. That's characteristically human; that's what makes us human. There's no limit to our ability to do those types of things.

So we're dealing with a single, global water system; but as we've been discussing on these shows, we're now at the point where we're looking at this more closely, we're re-approaching this thing we call the global water system. And we're realizing it's not really a *global* system: We're looking at a manifestation on the planet Earth, but what's being manifested is not fundamentally a phenomenon of the planet Earth itself. The global water system is an expression of cosmic principles, cosmic influences. It's an expression of the activity of the Solar System as a whole. The Sun is driving the

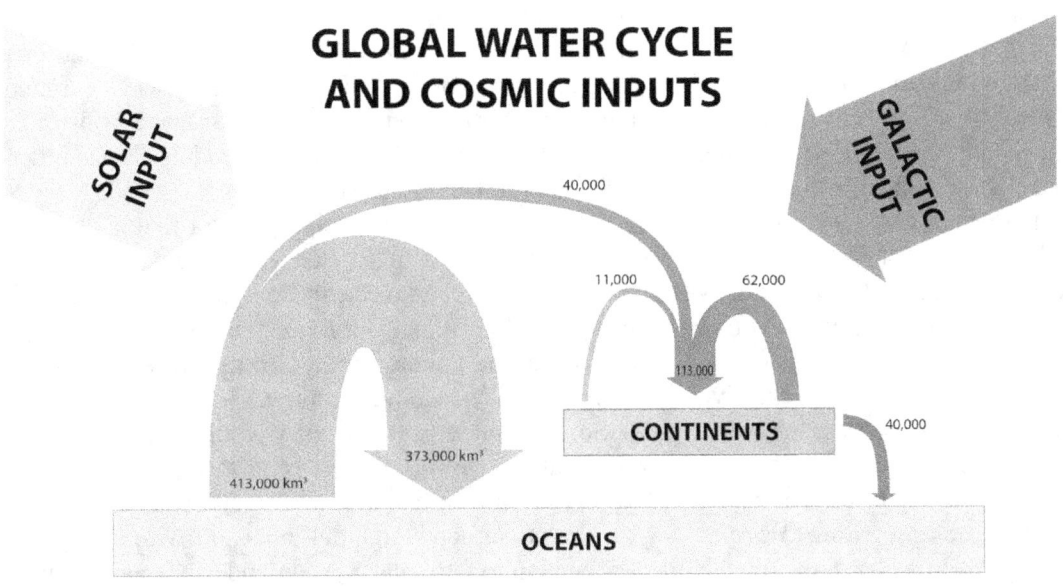

GLOBAL WATER CYCLE AND COSMIC INPUTS

SOLAR INPUT

GALACTIC INPUT

40,000

11,000   62,000

113,000

CONTINENTS   40,000

373,000 km³

413,000 km³

OCEANS

LPAC/Benjamin Deniston

What we think of as our global water cycle is really governed by principles of a higher, subsuming system—that of our Solar System's interaction with the galaxy. All flows are given in cubic kilometers of water per year.

the relationship of our Solar System to the galaxy. So that's our starting point now. That's our minimum, our baseline, for thinking about water, and about the water crisis.

Mankind's Intervention

This completely changes how we understand the issue of mankind's relationship to the water cycle. And this is not just an academic study. This is not just saying, "Okay so we observe that the galaxy has this influence, has this role," and then we go back to doing what we were doing before. This is the basis for a completely new level of how mankind is able to act on Earth managing the system, influenced and informed by this higher-level, higher-principled understanding of the water system as an expression of the solar-galactic relationship.

We've discussed these water modification technologies. They're just the beginning phases of mankind being able to manage these atmospheric conditions, these conditions associated with the role of galactic activity in the water cycle—that we can actually tap into the activity of the cycle as a whole, in a way that's informed by our understanding of the system being driven by these larger, galactic forces.

So this is now the start, this is the baseline from which we re-approach this question from this point onward. Now we recognize that what we're dealing with on Earth is not an Earth-based process, it's not defined by the Earth, it's not bounded to the Earth; it's an expression of these larger systems, these larger processes.

And here we are, now, mankind uniquely discovering this and defining this, and this gives us a completely new basis to act based on a higher-principled knowledge of the system as a whole. And this is what I want to emphasize here, and transition to what Jason [Ross] is going to go through on the issue, because this is what Mr. LaRouche was stressing earlier today: We have to solve the water crisis, but the way we're going to do that

entire process; the entire water system as we know it is powered and driven by the activity of the Sun, by nothing on Earth. So you're immediately dealing with the expression of something which is reflecting the process of the Solar System as a whole.

But what we're putting on the table, and what is really the challenge for those of us who choose to approach this crisis from the standpoint of being human, rather than animals, is that we now have insights into a higher-level understanding of this system, and it's not even just the Sun; it's not even just the Solar System, but the water cycle as we experience it, as we depend upon it, as we manage it, expresses the relationship between our Solar System and the galaxy more generally.

Now one of the most important influences affecting how the water system operates, especially in the atmospheric aspects of the cycle, is the role of galactic cosmic radiation, galactic factors, constantly affecting and determining the conditions of this supposedly Earth-based cycle.

What you see as the global water system, what we think we're dealing with, is really a phenomenon, as Mr. LaRouche was saying earlier this week—it's a phenomenon, but what are the principles? What's driving it, what are the causes? You see this expression, but now we're seeing that this expression itself is manifesting activity that's driven by these larger influences, by the activity of the Sun, by the activity of the galaxy more generally and is to understand that the crisis and the solutions as being expressed, encapsulated in this more fundamental issue of recognizing mankind as a fundamental force, not just on Earth, not an animal species on Earth, but a unique, creative force that can understand the Solar System, the principles governing the Solar System as a whole; that can begin to understand the principles governing this system of our galaxy and the relationship of our Solar System to our galaxy. And it's that new level of understanding which is *uniquely human*, that we can develop, and which gives us the ability to act differently, to create new actions on Earth, informed by this higher, creative understanding, which will allow us to address the water issues in a completely new way.

It's this unique perspective we have now, of being able to conceptualize the principles governing this relationship between our Earth to the Solar System, the Solar System to the galaxy, and then to use the science of that understanding to change how we act, to inform how we act, to allow us to act in a completely new way on Earth. *That* is human. That's uniquely human creative action, something Jerry Brown does not understand. And Mr. LaRouche was saying earlier today that the problem is that the supposed leaders don't understand this fundamental issue.

So this is now the underlying factor that we have to draw out, that we have to discuss, and to put up front and center. The way we handle these issues, the water crisis being a leading issue, is by a recognition of the unique capabilities of human creativity, as expressed in this water crisis as a leading example.

So, to transition to Jason, I would just say, if you want water—we're talking to California, now—if you want your water, if the Southwest states want their water, you have to understand mankind's ability to change his relationship to the Solar System and to the galaxy more broadly, and that takes us to an issue of human creativity, which Jason is going to discuss for us today.

Man's True Nature

by Jason Ross

Jason Ross of the LaRouchePAC Science Team gave this presentation to the weekly larouchepac.com webcast on April 24.

It's an undeniable, historical fact that the thinkers who created the Renaissance held the view that human beings are created in the image of God. We are creators and we carry the nature of the universe—its actual substance, the most characteristic basis upon which it operates—within us. Yet, clearly, most are unaware of this, unaware of both the nature of the creative potentials within their own minds, and of the nature of the universe itself.

Think about something that you know; have something in mind. We're used to the childlike question that comes up, "Why?" Children ask "Why?" You tell them an answer, and they ask "Why?" You answer that question, and you might be met with, "Why?" They realize they can go on like this for quite some time.

Ask another question: "How?"

How do you know whatever it is that you know? How do new things, known as discoveries, how do they become known to humanity? What is that process like—what is it as an experience internally, and what does it say about the nature and the action of us as a species? This experience, the creative process, is the most universal and essential of human experiences. It is a sense of the highest kind of goodness and love, as it is expressed by Diotima in Plato's *Symposium*.

Creation and Discovery

So what is it to create? And is creating different than discovering? Take the field of music: I don't think many people would say that Beethoven "discovered" his Ninth Symphony, that he was excavating, and then he found it inside a rock, that he cracked the rock in half, and there was the score to the Ninth Symphony. Clearly not. There's a lot of music that's been written, there are many ways of approaching things. We definitely *create* music. That's a human field.

What about another field, the seemingly different field of science? When scientists discover something about how the universe works, how nature works, have they *created* knowledge? Have they *discovered* knowledge that was already there in the universe around them? Is there a distinction?

I think most people would believe that we discover things that already exist, that there are principles in nature, that they cause things to operate and unfold in the way that they do; we discover those things, and now we know them. There's certainly something to that.

However, as Cusa emphasized, and as Kepler understood in the way that he approached his discoveries, it's also an act of creation. There are two aspects to that: One, is the creation of a new idea, in the formation of an hypothesis. This gets left out, or underplayed, in the typical science fair procedures that people follow in school, where they come up with problems and hypotheses, and independent and dependent variables, and results and conclusions. The most interesting aspect, is the creation of a hypothesis: What happens when that hypothesis is of a sort that's never before been experienced?

Take Kepler: Kepler was the first modern scientist; he was the first astrophysicist. He discovered how the planets move, and he did it, not by looking at movement, but by looking at movers. He had a physical hypothesis. It wasn't entirely right. In fact, to modern ears and eyes, it seems like it's almost entirely wrong, in the way that he explained how the Sun caused the planets to move. But what he did, is he took a physical approach; he created a hypothesis of how it was that the Sun, like a magnet, could be the cause of the motions of the planets; he followed that idea through. It resulted in a kind of motion for which no mathematics existed at the time, and wasn't to exist for nearly 100 years, when Leibniz created the infinitesimal calculus.

He took that concept, that hypothesis that he had, and he had to create motions of the planets, to see if that fit. When he looked at the planets overall, as a system, he had to create a hypothesis of the musicality of the planets, of their distances between each other, of their [orbital] eccentricities, with the view of answering: how would God have composed the Solar System in order that it would have characteristics in it that correspond to musical ones, from a human point of view?

Kepler created. He discovered; he created.

The evil Bertrand Russell, who tried to eliminate both creativity and people

Problems: Euclid and Russell

So, let's look at some problems in this, and then we'll come back to examining what this says about us as a species.

Let's take up one of the most ancient of problems, take Lyndon LaRouche's view of Euclid: LaRouche describes his first experiences with Euclid in school as a young man, as a student, as being not of the most pleasant variety. He really hated what Euclid had done, and it wasn't because he really disliked school or learning in general. Think about what the problem with Euclid was.

Euclid wrote these books about the *Elements of Geometry*, in which he has 13 books in which, starting from a few basic axioms of geometry, he derives a variety of properties of geometric constructions: cutting angles in half, the sum of the angles in polygons, eventually getting to the Platonic solids, things like that.

Here's the trouble with it: One, and this was recognized by Riemann and Einstein, Euclid's space was flat, even though space didn't have to be flat. But that's not the most glaring error, although it's an easier one to understand. The other error is that Euclid presented knowledge as deduction: that from a basic set of axioms—and it's not that many, about a dozen—you could derive the knowledge of everything that there would ever be to know about geometry.

Taking that as a model for knowledge more generally is poison. It's deadly, because discovery doesn't come from deducing conclusions from assumptions that we already have. You don't get to the future from the past. You don't get to a new concept, a new scientific principle, by showing how it's consistent and follows from what you already knew. More on that in a moment.

Gottfried Leibniz (1646–1716) developed the infinitesimal calculus, a language that allowed change itself to be substance.

Take another example: LaRouche has been emphatic about the destructive effects on science in the 20th Century, especially the role played by Bertrand Russell, in his promotion of an attempt by David Hilbert, in the very early 1900s, to do something that might seem so abstract or academic as to be unimportant, that its importance can be overlooked. Hilbert had proposed, as a study, to determine whether it was possible to turn mathematics (arithmetic, in particular) into logic. Was it possible to derive all of the properties of arithmetic—adding and multiplying and subtracting and dividing, and a few other things—was it possible to derive everything interesting about that, from *logic itself, from the deductive process?*

Bertrand Russell set off to do that. His book *The Principles of Mathematics*}, later written in Latin, the *Principia Mathematica*—the reference to Newton, I think, is clear there—where Russell attempted to redefine the way that logic worked, redefines the way that arithmetic worked, to make it possible to make mathematics a branch of logic. I think he thought he succeeded.

Kurt Gödel, a couple of decades later, after Russell's publication of this book, made a devastating proof—you may have heard of it; it's called "Gödel's proof," for short. It actually has a long, more technical title. Basically, what Gödel showed, was that in any sufficiently complex system, like the logic of arithmetic that Russell tried to create, it was always possible to cause that system to break apart, to make statements that were contradictory, or to make statements that were undecidable: There was always more to discover, than could *ever* be put in any system, where all future knowledge can be derived from the past. He showed that even in arithmetic, which doesn't seem like a very big scope—this doesn't include the mysteries of life or how the brain works, this is just arithmetic—that even in that limited field, the attempt to say that there's no creativity, and that knowledge can be derived from the past, from a few basic assumptions—even in that limited field, it failed.

This proved that artificial intelligence, before it had even really been created, was a waste of time. I don't think everybody who's working in that field, realizes that, however.

Overthrowing the Old System

So, with these examples, and with the importance that LaRouche has ascribed to them; with the problem of Euclid, which was overcome by Riemann, with the problem of Russell, and how Gödel fought against him; and to give one more example, the problems left by Kepler, about how change itself could be part of the language of science, this was resolved by Leibniz when he created his infinitesimal calculus. For the first time, it was possible, instead of things themselves, or relations among objects—*stuff*—instead of that being what was real, Leibniz allowed the way that those things changed, to itself have a real existence, and he developed a language that let change be discussed, directly. That was an amazing advancement.

What Bernhard Riemann did, in creating an anti-Euclidean geometry, was, in addition to showing that space didn't have to be flat, that there were a lot of three-dimensional manifolds that aren't necessarily flat like Euclid's space, such as later, Einstein's general relativity and curved space-time, Riemann also said: Look, the basis of our understanding of this, the basis for understanding the shape of space, isn't in geometry, it's in those physical principles that we discovered, that govern how things take place in space.

So with these things, we've got a couple of ideas

floating around now: one, the actual existence of change itself, as a concept; and two, the fact that the development of knowledge has *nothing in common* with logic, with deduction, with anything a computer can do. If you're a very logical person, you're never going to make a scientific discovery, because the universe is illogical. It's not random and unreasonable; but it is, absolutely and fundamentally, illogical.

So, how does that occur? We've discussed before—I'll be brief with it—with an example that V.I. Vernadsky gave in a 1930 paper, where he talked about how, thanks to the work of Planck and Einstein, the language of physics had dramatically changed over the preceding three decades. He gave the examples of the concepts of space and time, of energy and matter, which were totally different in his day, than in 1900: space and time used to be separate. According to Newton, they were independent things, they had no particular characteristics. Space was just a sort of galactic coordinate system in which different things would exist; time just flowed on its own, nothing special about it.

Einstein showed that there was only action in space-time, combined; that space had a shape to it, that time could vary in its duration, based on the motion of different observers watching a process unfold; and that even the concept of "now," of simultaneity, would be different for different observers. This totally blew apart those very basic concepts of space and time, which seemingly had been around for centuries. The other two, energy and matter—Einstein showed that energy could become matter and vice versa, this is what happens in nuclear processes. Planck showed that energy came in pieces, like the matter of atoms.

So, those examples show how, just at the beginning of the last century, the very basic language, the basic concepts used to even *discuss* the universe, all changed fundamentally—and not by additions, not by deriving something new to add to them, but by fundamentally *replacing, overthrowing, invalidating* the old concepts. Discoveries aren't additions: They always overthrow something that's wrong, because they're arrived at by a contradiction.

Man and the Developing Universe

The other aspect of this: What does it mean about us as a species, that we do this? How do we change the universe? How do we understand it?

First off, let's think about thought as a physical force. There are a lot of physical forces that are commonly

Vladimir Vernadsky, treating mankind as a scientific phenomenon, knew that the world view of Newton would have to give way to one in which thought itself was a physical force.

considered: gravity— people think about that—friction, magnetism, electricity flow, Ohm's law, springs, all these kinds of things.

We understand these in a way that's different from the animals. Take a dog. Now dogs try to understand things around them, and there are some things they can understand; they figure things out about the world around them; they try to train people in ways that they're susceptible of being trained.

We do something different, right? Our thoughts create things that have never existed before; thought is acting as a force of nature. Take an example from Vernadsky: aluminum. Pure aluminum, native aluminum, aluminum all by itself, not as a compound, exists *nowhere* in the Earth's crust. Well, now it does exist. But it didn't exist before people: We created something that never existed before on this planet.

Nuclear fission: Although the principle upon which it's based predated the 20th Century, the process of fission that takes place in a nuclear power plant doesn't occur anywhere on Earth (except perhaps one unusual

LaRouche references Raphael's School of Athens as representing a simultaneity of eternity, in which thinkers of different eras meet, outside of time.

that we've discovered, they're never actually, completely right. None of them is so right that it won't in the future have the potential of being replaced by a discovery that supersedes it, as in Vernadsky's reference to the early 20th Century, where everything was overthrown; all of the laws of physics were overthrown, and basically every one of them was replaced.

So, the fact that the universe develops, that it responds to our developing discoveries about it, and our ability to create new things in the universe that would not exist without us, I think bridges the gap between the notions of creativity and discovery: *We are creators.* That image from the Renaissance—that was absolutely a living image in the minds of those who created it, that human beings were made in the image of God. Think about that in modern terms.

The Experience of Discovery

So, let's talk about, what that world's like, that universe out there: How do we get there? How do we make discoveries about it?

As I think I've said, briefly, new insights into it always come from contradictions in our current understanding, overthrowing our old thoughts, by developing a new and necessary idea. Think about the experience of time, when we do that. You think about a timeline, as you might imagine it in a history book, or looking at geological ages; you know, time moves along. It moves from the past, into the present, and then into the future.

The thing is, when you introduce something that's new, the development of steam power for example, if you said humanity was on a timeline, well, was that an inevitable discovery? When that occurs, is that just the past going into the future? Or is that a willful creation of something that had never existed before, actually changing time, changing where we would be going? Acting on that process of moving into the future itself?

place in Africa, [Oklo in Gabon – ed.]) but overall it's a process that really just doesn't occur. Or consider the kind of fusion that we're working on creating in our laboratories. Although it's based on what we believe to be taking place in stars and other things, the way that we would be creating it, is something that's never happened before. Or coal burning and then producing motion: That doesn't happen without people.

So, thought is a power in the universe; if it weren't, then the universe would be fundamentally unreasonable. It wouldn't work internally, as something that *does* let us understand things about that world, and it wouldn't work externally, letting us transform ourselves as a species, increasing our, what you might call, "carrying capacity," as Ben had referenced, that we have transformed the potential population of our species. Animals haven't done that; they won't do it—they don't, unless there's other creative life somewhere else in the universe.

So, in this way, we're like the universe itself. The universe develops. Look at the development of life over evolutionary time on our planet; look at the new technologies, you might call them, that have been introduced. Look at the development of galaxies over time. And then think about people who are worried about entropy and the heat death of the universe, and you can discard that as a concept. The universe develops.

And, consider this: Our discoveries, those principles

I think it is.

And I think that that experience, the experience of discovery, the experience of the creative process, in science, or in developing a greater insight into music, poetry, etc., that in doing that, we get to experience that reality that lies outside of time. Mr. LaRouche has re-

---

This is something that's absolutely within our grasp. If the universe can do something, we can discover how it does it, and we can do it ourselves.

---

ferred to a "simultaneity of eternity," as seen in Raphael's *School of Athens* painting, where thinkers from different periods of history are all together. When you act on the trajectory of our species, and therefore the trajectory of the development of the universe itself, yes, it happens at a time, you might say, but the experience isn't one of being in time; it's being in eternity.

The greatest duty, or mission, or opportunity of so-

ciety, of government, is to provide the greatest number, an increasing number of its people, the opportunity to participate in a process that really is immortal, that goes beyond a lifetime, not only in the sense of being remembered, leaving an impact that can't be effaced, but in changing what that idea of the future even could be. That's been something that not that many people over history have been actively engaged in, and which, at an increased rate in a society that understands that as the nature of human beings, will be able to progress in ways that would seem unbelievable to us today.

It would certainly be a society where, going into space wouldn't be a difficulty; where controlling asteroids or comets that might destroy our planet, or at least life on it, wouldn't be out of the question; where we have fusion power, for power here on Earth, for transportation and as an energy source, for controlling the Solar System, and actions in it. It certainly wouldn't be one where we would worry about whether the Sun happened to evaporate water which we were then fortunate enough to have land in a place where we would want it. We don't do that with food presently: If there's no food in a farmer's field, he doesn't say, "Oh, there's a food crisis." His neighbor might say, "Well, you forgot to plant during the planting season, that's why there are no crops there now!"

With water, we can control the water cycles. This is something that's absolutely within our grasp. If the universe can do something, we can discover how it does it, and we can do it ourselves. Even on the very, very practical level—maybe this might bring it down a notch, but—even the amount of money that California was ripped off by the Enron fiasco around the year 2000, [$70 billion] that would be enough money to build desalination plants for all the metropolitan coastal areas of the state, for 25 million people: just the amount of money that was stolen during the Enron fiasco.

So, the kind of humanity that we need to create, the idea of culture that we ought to strive for and develop, and exist in and live as, is one where these problems are surmountable. These aren't things that we can't deal with.

And we'll be able to engage ourselves in more interesting problems: How does the Sun work? How is the galaxy developing in the way that it is? You know, fun things! New music, fun and exciting things. We won't have to worry about things like, why is the governor of California such an idiot?

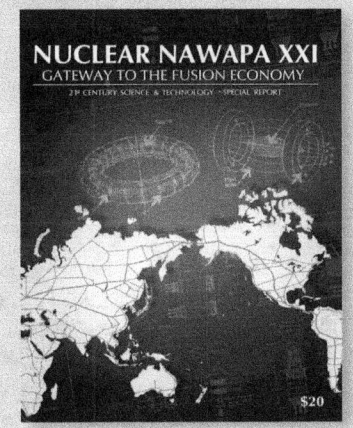

Two Systems: Russia's Role

by Helga Zepp-LaRouche

In a speech April 24 at the prestigious Cultural-Business Dialogue in Baden-Baden, Germany, Helga Zepp-LaRouche addressed the danger of the breakdown crisis of the Western financial system as well as that of a new world war. The alternative to that is the BRICS perspective, she said, which Europeans should seize upon to find a constructive way out of the crisis. That view is also held by many Americans, she stressed, who oppose the destructive geopolitics of the Obama Administration.

The Baden-Baden event was organized by the German-Russian Art Assembly association, It was addressed by senior officials of the Russian Foreign and Finance Ministries, as well as by leading figures of German-Russian economic relations, and by Prof. Shi Ze of the China Institute of International Studies in Beijing.

Though this may not be so obvious: Strategically, we must consider two completely different systems.

One system is based on geopolitical expansion, on monetarism, on maximization of the profits of a few. Should this system prevail, it may lead to the extinction of the human race.

Fortunately, there is an entirely different system, of which you of course have some knowledge, but you may not know the full scope: Namely, that a completely parallel economic and financial system has arisen since last July, one which certainly is not without its problems, but has an entirely different orientation; and indeed, is based on the future, and on human creativity.

This picture (**Figure 1**) is from the Fortaleza Summit of the BRICS nations in Brazil last year; and you see, standing next to President Putin, Narendra Modi, the Prime Minister of India. He said: The BRICS are the

FIGURE 1

FIGURE 2
Eurasia: Main Routes and Selected Secondary Routes of the Eurasian Land-Bridge

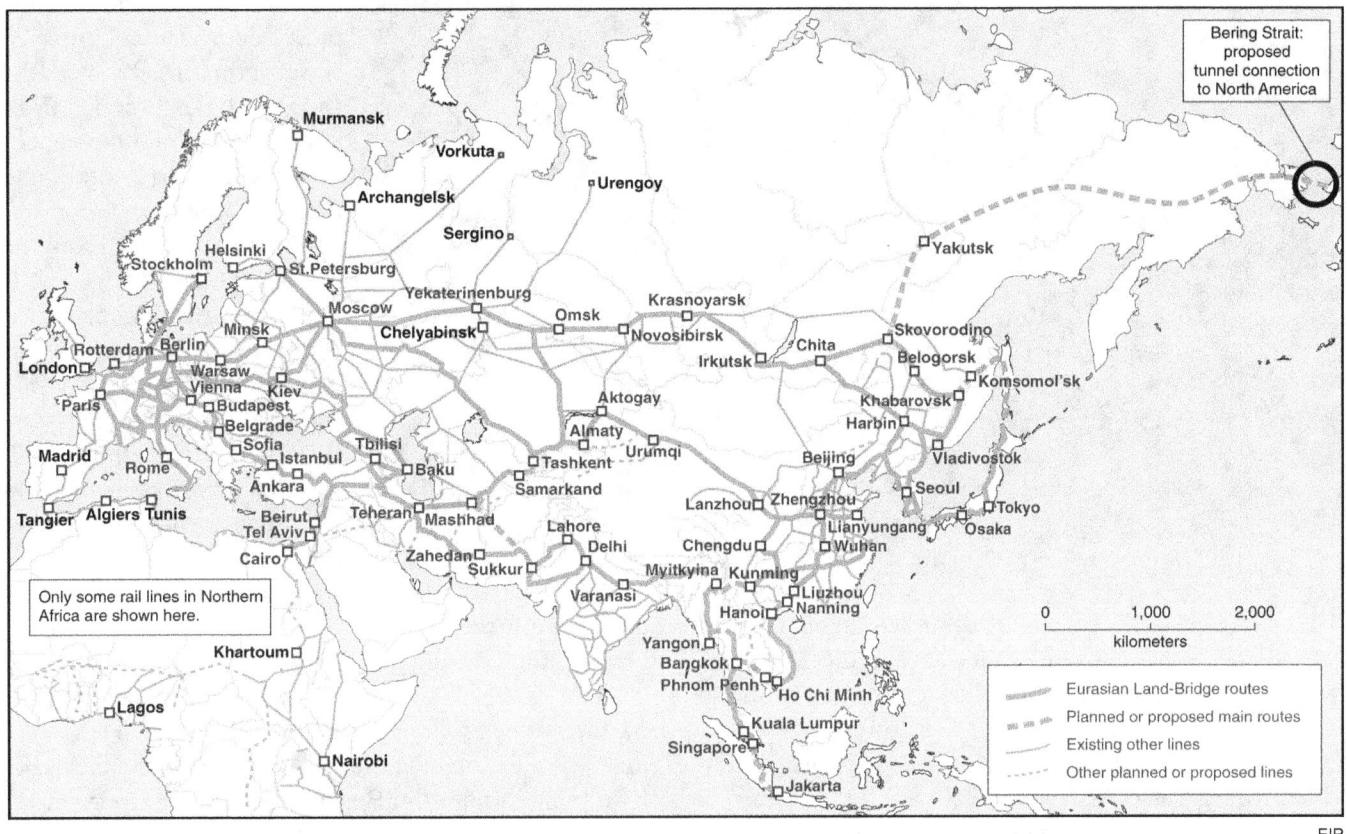

EIR

This map represents the schematic of the Eurasian Land-Bridge plan laid out by the Schiller Institute in the early 1990s. Compare this with the map of the status of today's Land-Bridge see Figure 9..

first alliance in the history of mankind which is defined not on the basis of present capacities, but by the future potential of all these nations.

Through the initiatives of Chinese President Xi Jinping, in particular, the New Silk Road and the Maritime Silk Road of the 21st Century form the framework of a new economic and financial system which is rapidly developing.

This includes, above all, a new financial system. It consists in the Asian Infrastructure Investment Bank, the New Development Bank, the Bank of the Shanghai Cooperation Organization, the bank of the SAARC nations, the New Silk Road Development Fund, and the Maritime Silk Road Fund. These banks represent a fundamental break with the casino economy of Wall Street and the City of London, because these banks are oriented exclusively to the development of the real economy, of the economic infrastructure and common welfare of their nations.

Xi Jinping has emphasized repeatedly: The new financial architecture is in no way a Chinese imperial competitor to the American imperial structure, but an inclusive concept in which all nations are to collaborate—America, the Europeans. This is a "win-win idea," for the mutual advantage of all who take part.

I say to you that our future existence as a human race, depends on succeeding in winning over America and Europe to cooperation with these BRICS nations.

Now some in Russia fear that China is too influential in this development, because, of course, it has had a huge economic development over the last 30 years. But I would like to demonstrate briefly that Russia has also played a major role, in the sphere of ideas, in bringing this new model into being.

The Future of Eurasia

This (**Figure 2**) is a plan for the Eurasian Land-Bridge, which we—the Schiller Institute—proposed in

FIGURE 3

But Lyndon LaRouche—my husband—and I were often in Russia, and presented these ideas. This (**Figure 3**) was a forum in 1995 with the former Soviet Premier [Valentin] Pavlov and the economists [Gennadi] Osipov and [Leonid] Abalkin.

This is a report on the Eurasian Land-Bridge, written by the Academician [Alexander] Miasnikov—this was in 1997—and Russian economists were already discussing this concept in 1997.

This (**Figure 4**) was a 2001 conference in honor of Pobisk Kuznetzov, and this was focused on why the ideas of Vladimir Vernadsky must dominate the Eurasian order of the future.

1991 after the Soviet Union had broken up, and which was conceived as a strategy for peace in the 21st Century, in which infrastructure corridors from Europe to Asia would be built.

As you know, this was not realized, because at that time, Margaret Thatcher and Bush Sr. wanted to reduce Russia from a superpower to a raw-materials-producing country, in which shock therapy was applied.

This is Academician Alexander Granberg (**Figure 5**), the father of the Bering Strait Crossing. That is the idea of connecting the Eurasian Landbridge with Alaska by a tunnel under the Bering Strait. It is important for the development of the Russian Far East, where the world's greatest reserves of raw materials lie under permafrost, untapped; and it is necessary to create conditions under which people who work there may also live there.

Thus, for example, such an Arctic city—Umka—has been planned as a model (**Figure 6**), and this is also a step toward development in space. For these domed cities in Siberia can also be the model for domed cities on the Moon, or later on other bodies of the Solar System.

[Deputy Prime Minister] Dmitri Rogozin has said, precisely on this point, that the BRICS nations are all spacefaring and cosmic nations, and therefore the future of humanity will be determined very powerfully by knowledge of the Solar System and of our galaxy.

Here you see (**Figure 7**) an image of the deserts which are now spreading extremely quickly across the world, all the

FIGURE 4

FIGURE 5

FIGURE 6

way from the Atlantic Coast of Africa to China, and of course in California and the American West.

The oligarchical model—the system that I described at the outset—speculates on water becoming constantly more scarce and being privatized, and that the greatest possible profits are to be made on scarce water. Wall Street has been buying up, during the past decade, everything having to do with water, worldwide: lakes, aquifers, water treatment chemicals, absolutely everything.

China, on the other hand, is the only country which has carried out large-scale water management programs: the Three Gorges Dam, which now generates 22.5 GW of hydropower, and which has saved the lives of many human beings; and the bringing of water from its source in the Yangtze Kiang to the North, which is desert.

FIGURE 7

MAJOR DESERTS

The Creative Species

But to really increase the scarce water supplies available to mankind, we must make use of events in the galaxy and the Solar System in order to produce more water. Here you see (**Figure 8**) a representation of the 32 million-year periods in which our Solar System undergoes a cyclical motion, moving above and

below the plane of the Milky Way. This has an enormous effect on the cosmic radiation, which leads to cloud formation, and which causes all precipitation by ionization of the moisture in the atmosphere. The conquest of space will also be enormously important in the

FIGURE 8

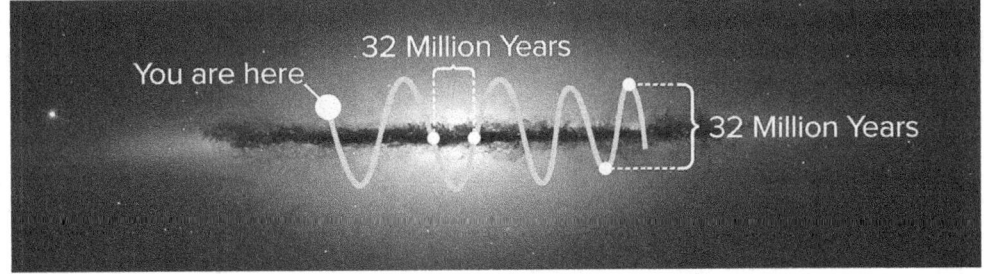

You are here   32 Million Years   32 Million Years

FIGURE 9

The World Land-Bridge Network—Key Links and Corridors

*Committed, underway or completed.

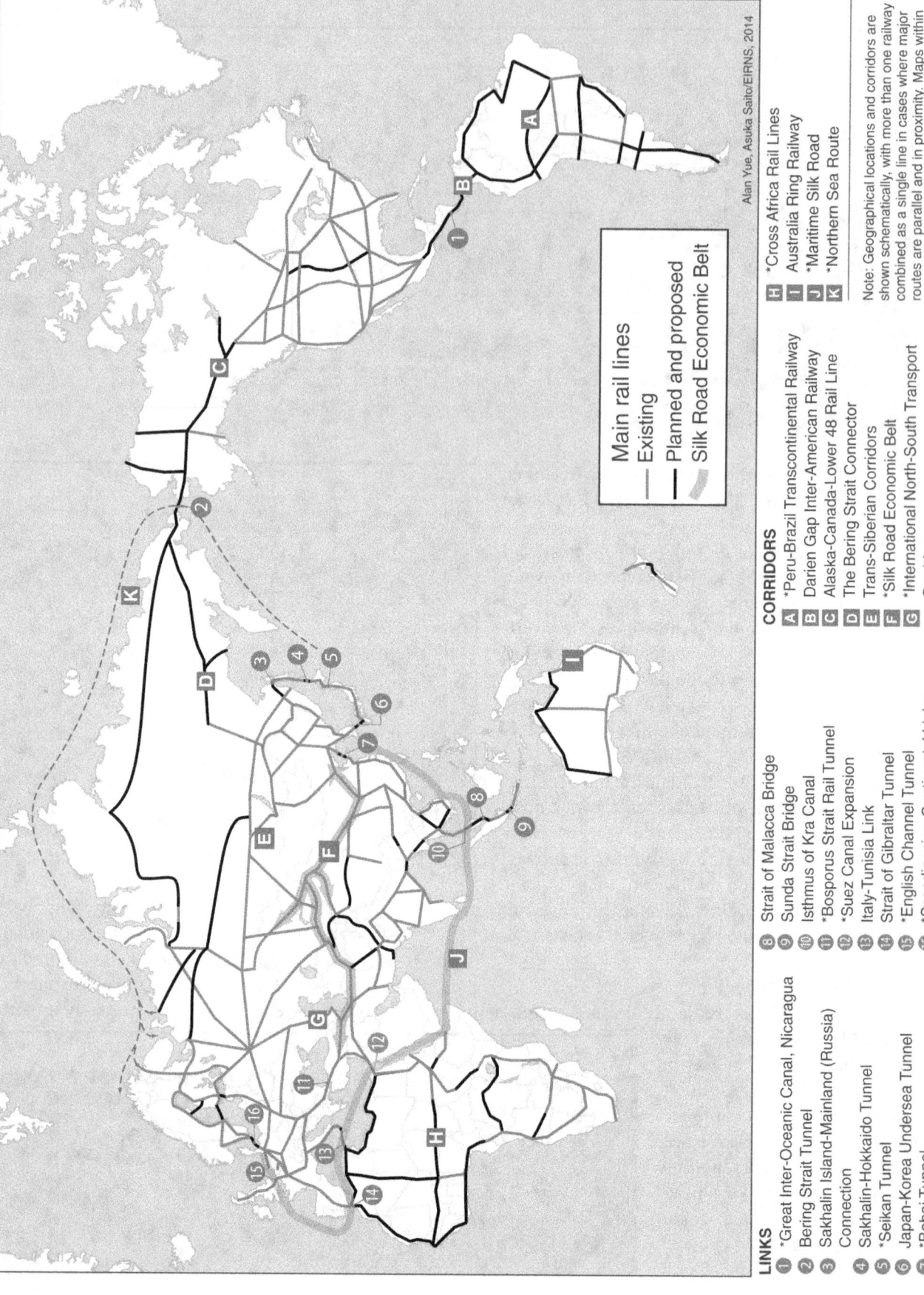

Alan Yue, Asuka Saito/EIRNS, 2014

Main rail lines
— Existing
— Planned and proposed
~ Silk Road Economic Belt

LINKS

1. *Great Inter-Oceanic Canal, Nicaragua
2. Bering Strait Tunnel
3. Sakhalin Island-Mainland (Russia) Connection
4. Sakhalin-Hokkaido Tunnel
5. *Seikan Tunnel
6. Japan-Korea Undersea Tunnel
7. *Bohai Tunnel
8. Strait of Malacca Bridge
9. Sunda Strait Bridge
10. Isthmus of Kra Canal
11. *Bosporus Strait Rail Tunnel
12. *Suez Canal Expansion
13. Italy-Tunisia Link
14. Strait of Gibraltar Tunnel
15. *English Channel Tunnel
16. *Scandinavian-Continental Links

CORRIDORS

A. *Peru-Brazil Transcontinental Railway
B. Darien Gap Inter-American Railway
C. Alaska-Canada-Lower 48 Rail Line
D. The Bering Strait Connector
E. Trans-Siberian Corridors
F. *Silk Road Economic Belt
G. *International North-South Transport Corridor
H. *Cross Africa Rail Lines
I. Australia Ring Railway
J. *Maritime Silk Road
K. *Northern Sea Route

Note: Geographical locations and corridors are shown schematically, with more than one railway combined as a single line in cases where major routes are parallel and in proximity. Maps within chapters of this report show greater detail.

FIGURE 10

future, for the conquest of problems on Earth.

In fact, the New Silk Road will conclude the last phase of infrastructure development on our planet, and the next phase will be the development of near-Earth space. And just as the old Silk Road brought economic welfare and exchange of culture and technology to all the populations along it, so the New Silk Road and the World Land-Bridge will have the same beneficial effect in enabling peoples to live together in harmony.

You see here the projects which will be combined in the World Land-Bridge, as a single international community. And the new economic order which will arise, will be determined— *must* be determined—by Vladimir Vernadsky's idea of the Noösphere, that realm in which the intellectual power and activity of human beings increasingly dominate the pure biosphere; that is, in which the human race truly develops toward reason. That is the precondition for our survival as the human race, as the creative species.

Here is an animation (**Figure 10**) of a future Moon colony. China is working on this in order to release

helium-3 from the Moon surface, for the future nuclear fusion economy on Earth. Once we achieve nuclear fusion, we have energy security—because the helium-3 on the Moon will suffice for some 10,000 years—and raw materials security, because we will then be able to convert raw materials by the fusion torch method to their ions, from which new raw materials can then be composed.

The employment of human creativity is all-important, because everything depends on whether we make the leap from a human race mostly still imprisoned in oligarchical thinking—greed, monetarism, desire for possessions—and change our identity to that of a creative humanity.

Human beings are the only creatures which are capable of constantly new thoughts, never thought before, which can redefine the identity of the human race in the cosmos. And that is the precondition for our being able to overcome our present dangers. I will be very grateful if you will concern yourselves with this question of creativity, because all of our lives depend upon it.

Can Democrats Revive the Presidency?

by Debra Hanania Freeman

April 24—Although the first of the primary elections to determine the 2016 Democratic Presidential nominee is more than nine months away, the fight to determine the policy standard that nominee must meet—and indeed the policy and fundamental principles that will shape the Presidency itself—continues to emerge with sharper clarity. As it does, it threatens to overturn the chessboard in what political commentators and pundits were touting as an inevitable Bush vs. Clinton national election.

Former Maryland Governor Martin O'Malley, who is expected to formally announce that he will seek the Democratic nomination sometime next month, has repeatedly stated that the reinstatement of the Glass-Steagall Act, dividing commercial and investment banking, is the single and most important first step that must be taken if the United States has any hope of restoring the U.S. economy. His insistence on this point in speaking engagements and press and media interviews across the nation has breathed a renewed sense of aggressiveness into the statements and activity of Massachusetts Senator Elizabeth Warren, long seen as the poster child for reducing the size and power Wall Street's Too-Big-To-Fail banks.

Together, O'Malley and Warren have come to define a new standard of leadership, setting off a virtual civil war inside the Democratic Party, and increasingly causing problems for Obama's attempts to ram Wall Street's "Final Solution" agenda through the Congress before he leaves office. The long-simmering divide erupted this past week, when Obama, working through the Republican leadership in both the Senate and the House, made an unprecedented attempt to ram through the "Fast Track" TPA—Trade Promotion Authority—preparatory to the Trans-Pacific Partnership. The bill gives Obama the ability to finalize trade deals like the TPP—itself an economic and strategic nightmare (see *EIR,* April 24, 2015) that could affect about 40% of the world's gross domestic product—and prevent lawmakers from making any changes, allowing them only an up-or-down vote.

A handful of Senate Democrats lined up behind Warren to oppose the legislation, saying they worry that it will ultimately do massive harm to already suffering American workers. And right now, all they can do is worry, since the details of the pact remain secret. Even Senate Minority Leader Harry Reid (D-Nev.), asked if he would support the legislation, said that "the answer is not only no, but hell no."

The Obama Administration has kept Wall Street well briefed on every aspect of the ongoing TPP negotiations, but has kept Congress largely in the dark. Members who have been briefed on the deal have been blocked by the administration from publicly discussing specifics. Last month, an administration official told the *Huffington Post* that negotiations on the deal were classified because "they were sensitive and ongoing."

O'Malley vs. Obama's 'Trade' Swindle

But on April 22, Warren accused the administration of deliberately hiding unpopular details from the public.

"The government doesn't want you to read this massive new trade agreement. It's top secret," Warren said in a statement on her website. "Why? Here's the real answer people have given me: 'We can't make this deal public because if the American people saw what was in it, they would be opposed to it.'

"If the American people would be opposed to a trade agreement if they saw it, then that agreement should not become the law of the United States," Warren continued.

Warren also said that there were provisions in the deal that would allow companies to ship jobs overseas, and weaken environmental or labor rules. The Massachusetts Senator also said that Congress should have the ability to amend the deal to get rid of objectionable provisions.

During an appearance on "The Rachel Maddow

Show" April 22, as the Senate Finance Committee voted 20-6 to pass the Fast Track authorization, Warren said that she worried that the authority Obama sought—to bypass Congress on the deal—could be used by future Presidents. Warren added that while ordinary citizens had been blocked from seeing the trade deal, businesses that could be affected by it were privy to details.

After the 20-16 vote in the Senate Finance Committee April 22, the Fast Track bill is expected to be approved by the full Senate within weeks.

But the question remains whether enough House Democrats will join with Republicans to pass the measure. On April 23, the House Ways and Means Committee passed "Fast Track" with a 25-13 vote; all the 13 "nays" were Democrats (out of 15 Dems on the Committee). Despite weeks of pounding by Administration officials, they voted *en masse* against Obama.

O'Malley, who has opposed the TPP as a bad deal all along, took a strong stand on the measure during an NPR interview April 20. When asked to elaborate his view, O'Malley said, "Yeah, I do oppose it. What's wrong with it is, first and foremost, that we're not allowed to read it before our representatives vote on it. What's wrong with it, is that right now what we should be doing are things that make our economy stronger here at home. And it's my concern that the Trans-Pacific Partnership—this deal which is urged by big corporations—many of whom have off-shored jobs, and many of whom have off-shored their profits—is bad for America's economy because it's bad for our middle class, and it is a race to the bottom, a chasing of lower wages abroad. And I believe that that does nothing to help us build a stronger economy here at home. And I am appalled by the notion that we're not allowed, as Americans, to read this agreement before our so-called representative institution of Congress votes on it."

After the Senate Finance Committee vote, O'Malley immediately posted his opposition on Twitter, and fired off an e-mail to supporters pledging his opposition to the Trans-Pacific Partnership. "To me, opposing bad trade deals like the TPP is just common sense," O'Malley wrote. "American workers whose jobs could be on the line right now, are owed more than lip-service. They deserve to know where leaders stand."

Whatever "leaders" could he be talking about?

It was a not-so-subtle swipe at Hillary Clinton, who is under increasing pressure from both fellow Democrats and the labor movement, to take a defini-

White House photo/Pete Sourza

Obama at Martha's Vineyard, August 2009

tive stance on the legislation. It's emerged as the first major policy dilemma of her Presidential bid, as she's faced with casting aside her own past as a free trade proponent (as Secretary of State, Clinton touted TPP as the "gold standard" of trade pacts), and publicly bucking Obama.

A growing number of Democratic lawmakers believe that a definite stance against Obama on this question, could be the factor that tips the scale. But the furthest Clinton has gone is to say in New Hampshire this week, "Any trade deal has to produce jobs, and raise wages, and increase prosperity, and protect our security," a statement that is simultaneously true and meaningless.

Sen. Jeff Merkley (D-Ore.) told *Politico* April 22, "I think now that she's officially declared for President, she should share with people how she feels about this." He's not alone. There are many others who agree, saying that Clinton owes it to voters—and to the Democratic Party—to explicitly spell out her views on such a critical issue.

The Glass-Steagall Qualification

On April 24, *Mother Jones* magazine posted the headline "Hillary Wants a Piece of the Elizabeth Warren Love Fest," but that Clinton refuses to respond to the key points of principle made by Warren (and O'Malley), namely, that megabanks must be downsized and Glass-Steagall reinstated.

The article notes that Clinton "penned a fawning blurb" on Warren for *Time* magazine's list of 2015's most influential people, but that her campaign refused to reply when *Mother Jones* supplied it with a list of seven Warren positions for comment. The list starts, 1) "Breaking up the largest banks and setting a cap on the size of banks; and 2) Reinstating the parts of the Glass-Steagall Act repealed during Bill Clinton's Presidency that required a separation between commercial and investment banking."

Two days earlier, on April 22, an e-mail blast went out from Americans for Financial Reform, identifying Glass-Steagall as one among their "no-nonsense set of proposals" which a Presidential candidate must "stand behind." The first of their four points calls for "Steps to reduce the size and power of the Too-Big-To-Fail banks, including restoration of the Glass-Steagall division between investment and commercial banking."

In a somewhat humorous piece in the April 21 issue of *Politico*, Jack Schafer wrote, "Thousands have run for President, but only one candidate has ever unrun for the office: Hillary Clinton. Ever since she finally announced her entry into the contest a couple of weeks ago, she has been unrunning with ferocity. First she road-tripped a minivan 1,000 miles from New York to Iowa to ... listen."

Why is Clinton unrunning? Schafer says, "Actively running for President at this point would be too politically damaging for Clinton. By actively running, she would have to declare herself for or against the current administration, something she doesn't want to do until it presents some advantage."

Clinton may hope to avoid the intense political debate that might rob her of Obama's political blessing as his anointed successor (a peculiar objective given the growing public hatred of the man), and perhaps more important, might rob her of the huge sums of money she is counting on from friends on Wall Street—funds she believes she needs to win the Presidency.

But that is an impossible strategy.

During a campaign stop in New Hampshire April 20, Clinton said that, after listening to people in Iowa and New Hampshire, she was "surprised" to find out how much small-business growth has slowed.

"It's not enough just to tread water," she said. "We need to get ahead and stay ahead, and people need to feel their work is being rewarded and that the deck is not stacked in favor of those at the top."

It was an inane statement. With the U.S. economy in a state of utter collapse and the income gap widening by the day, many wondered how she could possibly be "surprised." Moreover, what does that say about her qualifications for the Presidency in a time of crisis?

Obama Loses It

April 27—In a series of public statements on April 23 and 24, President Obama, in a fit of manic, narcissistic rage, accused his unnamed opponents of being "dishonest," for stating that the Trans-Pacific Partnership (TPP) was a secret deal, which would harm Americans. He added that the Democrats will just have to "trust" him, because he would never do anything that would harm working people!

This drew a sharp response from two of the Democratic Senators who are leading the fight against the TPP. In an open letter to Obama, dated April 25, Senators Elizabeth Warren (Mass.) and Sherrod Brown (Ohio), blasted Obama for calling them dishonest. They wrote that it is his administration that classified the text of the TPP, and has "kept it hidden from public view, thereby making it a secret deal."

They continued, saying that while the public has been kept in the dark, the CEOs of the "country's biggest corporations and their lobbyists already have had significant opportunities not only to read it, but to shape its terms." Thus, instead of a "robust political debate," on the free-trade pact, Congress has been "muzzled by classification rules," imposed by Obama himself.

This direct attack against Obama represents a potentially decisive shift, as the battle is not just over the Fast Track for the TPP, but for the heart and soul of the Democratic Party.

—*Harley Schlanger*

Jeb Bush in New Hampshire, April 19, 2015. "Some have gone so far as to say, that were she [Hillary Clinton] to somehow actually secure the nomination on her terms, it could very well lead to a Jeb Bush electoral victory."

But, even this weak-kneed level of implied complaint, was too much for Obama's ego to bear. Over the next three days, one administration spokesman after another—and then finally Obama himself—felt they had to take issue with Clinton.

It is clearly the case that if Clinton thinks she can skate through the campaign for the Democratic nomination with platitudes about the middle class, she is dead wrong. It is well known that she has made private commitments to various Democrats in Congress, that she would support the re-enactment of Glass-Steagall, if she were to seek the Democratic nomination; and there's no way for her to wriggle out of the fact that she is viewed as tied to Wall Street and tied to Obama.

An increasing number of leading Democrats not only see her current strategy as incompetent, but say that her refusal to break with Wall Street and Obama, means that her winning the nomination is anything but a sure thing, especially as the growing O'Malley-Warren wing of the party sets a new standard for the Democratic nominee.

Some have gone so far as to say, that were she to somehow actually secure the nomination on her terms, it could very well lead to a Jeb Bush electoral victory. That isn't her plan, but at the moment, Hillary Clinton seems to be stupidly blinded by her own ambition.

www.ingramcontent.com/pod-product-compliance
Lightning Source LLC
Chambersburg PA
CBHW081004290526

45795CB00009B/3068